THIS BOOK BELONGS TO

....

THE
Crone
Zone

THE
Crone
Zone

HOW TO GET OLDER
WITH STYLE, NERVE, AND
A LITTLE BIT OF MAGIC

Nina Bargiel

QUIRK BOOKS
PHILADELPHIA

Full Library of Congress Cataloging-in-Publication Data available upon request.

ISBN: 978-1-68369-483-0

Printed in China

Typeset in Figtree, Manofa, Minion Pro, and Piazzolla

Designed by Paige Graff

Illustrations by Pam Wishbow

Production management by Mandy Sampson

Quirk Books
215 Church Street
Philadelphia, PA 19106
quirkbooks.com

Quirk Books' authorized representative in the EU for product safety and compliance is Easy Access System Europe, Mustamäe tee 50, 10621 Tallinn, Estonia, gpsr.requests@easproject.com.

10 9 8 7 6 5 4 3 2 1

"A witch ought never to be frightened in the darkest forest,
Granny Weatherwax had once told her,
because she should be sure in her soul that
the most terrifying thing in the forest was her."

—TERRY PRATCHETT, *WINTERSMITH*

Contents

Introduction

Welcome to the Crone Zone

Picture the crone: a gnarled old woman clad in a tattered black cloak. Stringy gray hair hangs limply over her shoulders, which are stooped with age. Her eyes are rheumy but all-seeing, hinting at the wisdom that lies within. She possesses magic found only in the dark heart of the woods. Legend has it she curses the souls of lost travelers and bakes children into pies. She prefers a solitary existence, rarely venturing into sight. But when she does, it is a fearsome harbinger of things to come.

The crone doesn't always show up as a hag. Sometimes she's a caretaker like Strega Nona, the Italian granny who doles out advice as well as bowls of pasta from her magical pot. But whether gracious grandmother or wicked witch, the crone is always cast as a woman whose best days are behind her.

At least, that's how people, especially men, have described her.

The crone archetype has been around for centuries, but she's most often associated with the three-faced Greek goddess Hecate. Hecate's three faces are said to represent the three phases of a woman's life: maiden, mother, and crone. Except that's not how she was perceived by the ancient Greeks, who saw her three aspects as more representative of birth, life, and death. The "crone" business didn't show up until *the mid-twentieth century*. In his books *The White Goddess* and *The Greek Myths*, poet and mythographer Robert Graves rebranded Hecate's faces as, let's be honest, the three types of woman our culture recognizes: "young and hot," "mommy," and "old and useless." In other words, you can be a **fucking goddess for more than two thousand years**, and one day some guy comes along and decides, *nah, she's a crone*. And that's that.

If it can happen to Hecate, it can happen to any of us—and it does. We spend our lives trying to fulfill all the expectations that society places on us, or that we place on ourselves: to be flawless but approachable, hot but also nurturing, competent enough to take care of everyone but never intimidating. And no matter how well we do at striking this impossible balance, one day everyone starts treating us like a hag who lives in a bog.

This book is for all of us entering our crone era—and looking to decide for ourselves what that means. Think of it less as a midlife crisis and more as a midlife calling. As we cross the threshold into cronedom, everything in our lives is changing—our goals, our fears, our living situations, our tolerance for bullshit, and especially our bodies. We stand at the crossroads with half our life behind us, trying not to pee, asking *is that all there is?*

While this book can't answer that for you, it can give you a place to start. On these pages you'll find crone wisdom and crone warnings, crone spells and crone inspiration. While I'll call upon pagan imagery and witchy ritual, this is not a book of witchcraft—but that's not to say you won't find some magic between its covers. You'll get to know me: Nina, your crone guide. And together, we'll discover our crone superpowers and learn about our crone touchstones:

Wisdom, to know who we are
Knowledge, to understand what we want
Fuck It, to do what we please

I don't know about you, but my crone era has lit a fire in me. It feels almost primal, like the power of a thousand *fuck its* has been flowing through my veins since birth and now is ready to be unleashed upon the world. I am a volcano, ready to erupt: **Mount St. Fuck You.**

Picture the crone: filled with power and fury. Picture the crone: filled with wisdom and knowledge. Picture the crone: filled with love and desire. Picture the crone: free.

Okay, crones. We're going in.

1

I, CRONE

Are you having feelings about getting older? Because I am. The person bagging my groceries calls me "ma'am." I have to scroll farther and farther to find my birth year each time I register for a free trial on Peacock that I'll forget to cancel. I get targeted ads on social media for AARP, walk-in tubs, and thick, comfy nonslip socks. (The socks are great, not gonna lie.)

But the weirdest part of aging—the part my brain still can't quite wrap itself around—is my changing face. Every morning I pad to the bathroom and am shocked by the stranger in the mirror. The creases that snake across her forehead are a little deeper in the morning light. Her laugh lines don't disappear when she stops laughing. And what the hell is going on with her neck?

It's got me thinking about another mirror: the Evil Queen's Magic Mirror, from *Snow White and the Seven Dwarfs*.

Snow White was my favorite Disney princess growing up. Mostly because she encapsulated the three things I wanted most out of life: disappearing into the forest, the ability to talk to animals, and a really good nap.

But as I've gotten older (fifty-one as of this writing), my affections have strayed from the perfect princess to the much more relatable ruler—the Evil Queen, Snow White's nemesis and the villain of the movie. Every day, like me, the Evil Queen looks into her mirror, and every day she asks: **"Who is the fairest one of all?"**

Sure, it's probably not 6:38 a.m., and the Evil Queen probably wasn't woken up by her bladder screaming *pee now, or we're gonna have a problem.* Also, her mirror is magic. But like me, the queen is aware of the passage of time. She's not asking the mirror who's the fairest just so she can get an ego boost. The queen is asking because she knows the drill: her power and position are intrinsically linked to her beauty. Without them, she has nothing. It's obvious that this is a competition and there is room for only one woman at the top, thank you very much. She needs to make sure every day that it's still her.

And it is, until one day it isn't. Suddenly, she's aged out of being the head bitch in charge, and the new woman at the top is Snow White. So what does the Evil Queen do? Does she push back against cultural norms? Does she tell everyone in the kingdom to go fuck themselves and dissolve the monarchy? No, she tricks Snow White into eating a poisoned apple, causing her to fall into a coma. It's a bit of an overcorrection. And I do not endorse this tactic! But can you blame her? The woman has been driven mad by the constant drumbeat of the Magic Mirror's judgment. Every single day this sad piece of glass that could have done something useful with its life, like be a champagne coupe, reminds the queen—the QUEEN!—that her value lies only in her youth and her beauty. I'm honestly shocked that the mirror wasn't selling poison apples as a side hustle.

The queen knows she has to disguise herself in order to get Snow White to take the poisoned apple. So she transforms herself . . . into a crone. The hideous crone, with her hunchback and stringy white hair, tattered black cloak and toothless maw. She's a little bit scary—if you take the time to notice her—but she's sad enough that she flies under the radar. And it works, kind of. Snow White eats the apple and the queen is on top again. But at what cost, and for how long?

You and I both know this plan is shortsighted. Sure, the queen manages to clutch onto the fairest spot for one more day. But what then? There's always another Snow White.

The funny thing is that the queen was so close to the answer. But it wasn't in the Magic Mirror.

The Evil Queen's fear is that she'll lose her power if she's no longer the "fairest one of all." But she transforms into a crone because **the crone can get one over on Snow White**, the woman currently sitting pretty on the top of the fairest heap. The queen understood that the crone has power—*more* power than just being the hottest bitch in the land. But she was too busy listening to the Magic Mirror to embrace it.

You might not be feeling like the fairest one of all. You may be mired in self-doubt. You may feel like you have nothing to say. But understand that it's the Magic Mirror's job to make you feel that way. Because you are *filled* with power: the power that comes from a lifetime of wisdom and experience. From the ability to not care what other people think. And from the desire to live the rest of our lives on our own terms.

Think of patriarchy as that evil mirror. It will trivialize your knowledge. It will belittle your self-worth. It will call you ugly, or dried-up, or a crazy cat lady. Because you are the mirror's worst nightmare:

A woman who no longer listens to a fucking mirror.

IN THIS CHAPTER, WE'LL LEARN:

* How to free yourself from the trap of productivity and embrace being useless
* How to find your crone voice
* How to create space for solitude
* More about your crone touchstones and how to use them
* How to develop and use your crone superpowers

Make Yourself Useless

Did you have one of those classic grannies? You know the type: She raised six kids. She made pie crust from scratch. Every year she cooked Thanksgiving dinner for seventeen people—with no dishwasher. She got up early and stayed up late. And even if she had a job outside the home, she kept that house spotless.

Tales of classic grannies are generally told with a touch of reverence, sometimes even wistfulness. Sure, Grandma was old, but she believed caring for her family was a sacred duty. A duty that lasted until death.

Maybe Grandma loved that sacred duty. Maybe she was truly fulfilled by the work. Maybe all she wanted out of life was to serve those around her.

Or maybe Grandma was programmed from birth to perform this sacred duty. Maybe she was taught that rest was selfish, something to indulge in only when she pushed herself to exhaustion or injury. Maybe Grandma put everyone else's needs before her own because she felt it was the only way to prove her worth in a world that considered old women unworthy. Maybe Grandma didn't have a choice.

It's not shocking that women feel like they have to take care of everything. Women are the ones who have historically shouldered the brunt of household labor. Then second-wave feminism hit, and women were allowed to have careers—as long as we still cleaned the house, watched the kids, and had dinner on the table at six-thirty every night. It was called Having It All! And it was possible, if you spent all your time and energy *doing* it all. (Uppers were also still legal and frequently prescribed.)

Honestly, it doesn't feel like anything's really changed. Sure, we're more aware of the problem. We talk about it more. But while everyone's sitting around discussing the fair and equitable division of household chores and child-rearing, women are pretty much the ones still doing it. And those discussions about the unjust division of labor tend to be followed by promises from men to be better, do more, and step up . . . as long as women tell them where to start.

It's not entirely men's fault. The blame lies in the belly of the beast itself: capitalism. And now it comes in extra-strength, thanks to hustle culture. If capitalism loves to link our personal and professional productivity to our worth as human beings, hustle culture cranks up that idea to eleven. Every mom has the same twenty-four hours, so why don't you have ripped abs fourteen hours after giving birth? It's not that the housing market tanked, it's that you have no work ethic. It's not that the job market sucks, it's that you're a lazy millennial. Forget inflation, student debt, and the wage gap. It's not a failure of the system you live in. Oh, no. It's all yours.

This is more connected to no longer being "the fairest one of all" than you might think. You know how society starts treating women as invisible once they're over fifty . . . or forty . . . or, let's be real, thirty-five? In part this happens because we're no longer considered fuckable, and we're considered unfuckable because we dared to age. But there's a larger story behind our disappearance . . . and an even bigger villain. That's right: it's capitalism again! When we're no longer seen as *useful* or *productive*—which can mean fuckable, but can also refer to the other things society believes women are "for," like raising kids or maintaining a household—we are simply no longer considered. It doesn't matter if we're working or pursuing our passions. Nope, the second we cross some arbitrary age threshold, we're no longer thought of as meaningful contributors to society. (That's reserved for billionaires who don't pay taxes.)

So how do we fight this?

We don't. (It was a trick question.)

Your instinct might be to work your ass off to show society, your boss, Jeff from accounting, and everyone else that you *are* useful! You *are* productive! But not only is hustle culture bullshit, you will never be able to prove your worth to a system that inherently thinks you're unworthy.

So, crones, we're not going to change *their* minds. We're going to change *ours*. We're going to learn how to divorce our sense of worth from our productivity. And we're going to do that by practicing being useless. We are going to marshal our decades of wisdom and knowledge and channel it into doing absolutely nothing for anyone else. We are gathering all of our *fuck it*s and heading to our cottage in the woods to drink tea, read dusty books, and befriend cartoon mice. At least metaphorically.

USEFUL TIPS FOR BEING USELESS

* **Just say no.** Take a failed 1980s drug policy and turn it into a personal mantra. Practice saying *no* to something once a day. Want extra credit? Say no and do not explain yourself. Just no. Full stop. Double points if you don't apologize!
* **Don't volunteer for things you don't want to do in the first place.** It's not your job to take care of everything. Really. Someone else can pick up the slack. And just because you have the time doesn't mean you are obligated to use it in service to someone else.
* **Make time for nothing.** If you're a scheduler, mark off time in your calendar to do nothing. It's as important as anything else on your to-do list.
* **Cut yourself some slack.** You're probably going to feel guilty. That's okay! It's going to take time to figure out how to make uselessness work for you. Don't feel bad about feeling bad.
* **Don't call them "guilty pleasures."** Stop apologizing about the things you enjoy. You're allowed to enjoy things. Is this change just semantics? Perhaps. But sometimes it feels like denying ourselves is the one hobby all women share. (Diet culture, anyone?) It's almost as if we feel bad about the things that make us happy, because it's not our job to be happy. Our job is to make others happy. Well, enough of that! No more guilt in your pleasures. (If you have passions you should actually feel bad about, like

cockfighting or fraud, that is beyond the scope of this book. But honestly, calling them "guilty pleasures" still won't *help*.)

* **Schedule a ditch day.** Most of us can't afford to go full *Eat, Pray, Love*. But maybe try Snack, Nap, Indulge. Take a day off every so often. Or an afternoon. The goal is to release yourself from your earthly obligations and create time that is completely your own. Read a book. Take yourself out for a glass of wine or a fancy tea. Disappear into the woods with your small army of squirrels.

Now, opting out of *all* of life's responsibilities is unrealistic for most of us. Even being able to take a step back comes from a position of privilege. And while it's important to prioritize your leisure, you also don't want to let down people who are truly dependent on you, or blithely peace out of the issues facing your communities. So where's the line between embracing uselessness and abdicating your responsibilities? It depends. If you need to, ask yourself a few questions before making the decision to say no:

* Is the task serious?
* Does it have to be done now?
* Am I the only one who can do it?
* Will something terrible happen if I don't do it (or don't do it right now)?

If you're North Carolina's best orthopedic surgeon, ripping off your scrubs and screaming "I'M PRACTICING USELESSNESS!" as you flee the operating room is probably not a great idea. Pretending you don't know how to make coffee when the coffee pot is empty in the doctor's lounge and you are *always* the one who does it because all the male doctors act like they suddenly don't have hands? Go ahead and be useless! (But maybe pick it up once in a while, out of community spirit.)

Let's Sit a Spell

Throughout this book (starting right now), you'll see spells, meditations, and rituals. If you haven't encountered spells before, rest assured that you don't need to subscribe to any specific belief system to use the ones in this book (although many religions and traditions do work with spells). Outside of a religious context, spells are all about intention, specifically:

1. Creating an intention.
2. Focusing or visualizing that intention.
3. Releasing that intention into the universe.

We're not summoning spirits here, or messing with the metaphysical. But there's still power in the practice of casting spells, because there's power in being able to articulate your intentions—or even just figure out what your intentions are! So you don't need to feel any sort of way about spirituality, magic, or religion. We're just getting to the heart of who you are and what you want.

 Free the Crone

When I started therapy in 2019, the first thing my therapist said was that I used *should* a lot. *I should eat healthier. I should work out more. I should be more patient. I should call my parents more.* No one was asking me to do any of those things (not even my parents!). But when I didn't live up to the expectations I had set for myself, I felt terrible. I was neck deep and drowning in the "shoulds." This is a "freedom from" spell, to rid yourself of all of your shoulds.

YOU'LL NEED

* Something to write on—this could be a notecard, or a piece of paper that outlines your responsibility (bills work great here!)
* Something to write with
* A fire-safe bowl
* A white candle (votives or sturdy pillar candles work best)
* Matches or a lighter

THE RITUAL

1. List your shoulds on your notecard or paper.
2. Place it in the bowl. (If it's too large, fold it to make it smaller.)
3. Light your candle, then use it to set the list in your bowl on fire. As always, please be careful when working with fire!
4. As the paper in your bowl burns, say: "I release myself from expectations. I release myself from fear." (Repeat as often as you'd like.)
5. When your list has turned to ash, finish by saying "I am free from, so I am free to."
6. Dispose of the ashes by planting them in your garden or simply tossing them out. (Make sure the ashes are completely cool first!)

We Care a Lot

Most of us have spent our lives being defined by the roles we play for the people around us: Daughter. Wife. Mom. It's like a Voltron of caretaking expectations. Obviously women don't have a monopoly on the caretaking experience—anyone of any gender can find themselves caring for a child, spouse, or parent. But the default is set to women, and even if the responsibility is shared, we're often still carrying a heavier load than others.

Our caretaker roles are so baked into the societal ether that we can't even escape them by going to work! Thousands of words have been written about how women do more office housework: making coffee, ordering lunch, taking up the collection for the office birthday gift. Plus we're expected to assume secretarial tasks that may not be part of our jobs: taking meeting notes, distributing agendas, scheduling meeting rooms. A lot of us just do it. (The book *The No Club: Putting a Stop to Women's Dead-End Work* refers to this as "non-promotable work"—work that not only won't garner us a promotion but distracts us from work that will.) And I get it. It's difficult to say no—especially to a boss or manager, but also to that little Magic Mirror voice in your head that tells you to be helpful and pleasant.

I've been in a bunch of television writers' rooms over my twenty-plus-year career. A writers' room is where writers gather to pitch episodes and write scripts. Snacks are a big part of the process. After an eight (okay, ten to fourteen) hour day, the table is littered with empty candy wrappers, crumpled napkins, doodles on sticky notes . . . it's a sea of garbage. In almost every single writers' room I've worked in, at the end of these long days, the men simply get up and leave the table. And the women? The women stay behind and clean it up—even women who are higher-ranking writers than the men. On one job, I dared to suggest that we all clean up after ourselves. I was called "The Housekeeping Police" and my contract wasn't renewed. Fun!

Since adolescence (or even before) we've been inundated with the message that it is our job to prioritize other people's comfort above our own—especially men's. And it's not limited to the men we know—it also applies to men who are complete strangers! It doesn't matter if you're in the grocery store, waiting for a colonoscopy, studying at the library, or performing a blood ritual under a new moon. Patriarchy reminds us to make way on the sidewalk. To smile politely. To clean up someone else's discarded candy wrappers from the table in the writers' room even though it's 1:17 a.m. and he ate all the strawberry Starburst.

But one day, you're just going to be done. One day, you're going to realize you've spent the last twenty years making sure everyone else is okay, without ever stopping to ask if you are. One day, you're going to leave the candy wrappers on his chair.

And that's the day you find your crone voice.

DO YOU HEAR YOURSELF?

Your crone voice is the most important tool in your magical arsenal. It's our new governing body, installed after our three touchstones—**Wisdom, Knowledge,** and **Fuck It**—stage a coup against all the patriarchal messages that we've been raised with. Your crone voice cuts through the bullshit. She (or he, or they, whatever feels right to you) comes right out and says what she wants instead of suggesting it. She's not self-important or needlessly demanding, but she will speak up and speak out when the situation requires it. She is the fierce, beating heart of your crone era.

We've been taught to stifle our crone voices, under the guise of "politeness" and "respectability," two ideas that have long been used to silence women—especially women of color. Politeness and respectability are tools used to discourage us from challenging the status quo. The crone prefers integrity and compassion over decorum.

All my life, I have been told I was too loud. So I made myself quieter. I was told I took up too much space. So I made myself smaller. I was told I was too much. And so I made myself less. I wish I had my crone voice back then. But she's here now. And she's way too much—and proud of it.

 # Release the Crone Voice!

This is a non-meditation meditation. An anti-meditation, if you will. We're going to go back to a time when we had to swallow our words in order to be polite. Our intention is to find our crone voice and yank her straight out of our hearts, bloody and warm. (Too much?)

YOU'LL NEED

* Your alone space (see page 27 for more). This is a spell that's probably best not performed in public, but don't worry, I'll give you options.
* An image of someone (or something) who's wronged you in a way you couldn't do anything about. A coworker who passed off your work as their own, but they were the boss's favorite. An in-law who insulted you to your face, but your spouse begged you to keep the peace. Patriarchy (self-explanatory). Mitch McConnell (see previous). This doesn't have to be a photograph—a labeled stick figure is plenty.
* Pen
* A calming drink, such as hot tea or a cocktail

THE RITUAL

1. Gather your items and sit down in your alone space. Stare at the picture of the person (or thing) who wronged you.
2. What do you really want to say to the person? It can specifically address the situation ("you stole my work, you useless bag of hair!") or just be a mean insult, as long as it's not a slur. I'm 100 percent sure your crone voice would not call anyone a slur. If you want to make up

insults, a four-letter word plus an animal or creature is a good formula (fuckgoblin, shithorse).

3. Grab your pen and scribble your word or message all over the image. Write it big, write it small, write it over and over, front and back—it's up to you.

4. If you are in a place where it is safe to do so, stand up and yell what you want to say as loud as you can! Or just scream like a hellbeast! (If you're in public, just imagine this part.) Rip the image to shreds.

5. Sit down and take three cleansing breaths. Then consume your calming drink. Congrats, crone. You found your voice!

Crone Alone

Greta Garbo is one of the most famous actresses from Hollywood's silent and golden eras. While her career began in her native Sweden, in 1925, MGM cofounder Louis Mayer brought her to the states to work for the studio. Garbo found huge success in America, but in 1948 she retired from the silver screen, opting to quietly (and privately) live out her life until her death in 1990.

Garbo's life and career were the stuff of legend: she was nominated for Oscars but never showed up to the ceremony. She didn't exactly hide her affairs with women. And she essentially became a recluse. Her quote from the 1932 film *Grand Hotel* became synonymous with her life: "I want to be alone."

The quote is a line of dialogue from Garbo's Grusinskaya, a Russian ballerina whose glory days are in the past. (Ballerinas, like actresses, get shuffled into cronehood earlier than other people—Garbo reportedly worried that, at twenty-seven, she was too old to play a dancer.) Grusinskaya, who is contemplating suicide, wants to be left alone with her memories and her despair. But when Garbo receded from the public eye, it was not to die but to live. Grusinskaya whines "I want to be alone" like a pouting kitten. But we can imagine Garbo saying it with her whole chest.

Garbo wasn't actually alone after she disappeared from Hollywood. She had close friends. She took lovers. But after years of belonging to the studio, to the audience, and to the role, the only person Garbo wanted to belong to was herself. She listened to her crone voice, the one that told her to take the space to live as she wanted, without apology. Crone goals.

I WANT TO BE ALONE

In 2017, I started to feel "off." At first, I blamed it on perimenopause. Over the next two years, I got physicals, checked and rechecked hormones, attended therapy and meditated and medicated. But it was like one of the chestbursters from *Alien* had taken residence in my rib cage. Every day I could feel the monster grow, increasing its stranglehold around my heart. My spouse of twelve years grew increasingly frustrated. But the more they pressed, the more I felt like the monster was going to explode out of me. I couldn't breathe. I needed to escape. I needed to sort out my head. I needed, like Grusinskaya and Garbo, to be alone.

So in the summer of 2019, I ran away from home. I took a solo road trip, driving from Los Angeles to my childhood home in the Midwest. As I passed through Utah, I felt the dark monster stir. It relaxed its grip around my heart and began to shrink as we passed under the red rock formations towering over the road. And it was at a Kum & Go gas station past Lincoln, Nebraska, that I realized that I didn't want to be married anymore.

And then the monster that had lived in my chest for the last two years was gone.

I felt sick hurting the person that I had once loved much more than myself.

But I also knew that I had spent the last two years trying to stifle the voice inside me. And instead of going away, it spread through my heart like a fungus.

When I told my spouse I wanted a divorce they said, "You're going die alone."

I'm sure they said it because they were hurt, and were trying to hurt me. However, I couldn't argue. I probably was going to spend the rest of my life alone. Unmarried. A divorcée! (Which is a fabulous word that we should bring back.) But being alone didn't scare me. Being lonely was the scary part. I wanted the loneliness to end.

I had been lonely before. Hell, I had been lonely my entire life. I was a weird, solitary kid. It goes with the territory. I befriended that feeling, and eventually loneliness taught me how to be happily alone. But being lonely in a marriage? There was no befriending that feeling. It was a dark, confusing place, a tornado alley of self-doubt and self-hate and hurt feelings. The funnel pulls you in and spins you around until you don't know which side is up, and then it spits you out somewhere new—and worse.

So I was going to die alone. And I was thrilled.

HELLO, DARKNESS! MY OLD FRIEND!

If we set aside *ugly* (we'll talk about this one later), the worst insults you can aim at a woman are supposed to be *single* and *lonely*. Whether she's alone by choice or by circumstance, the solitary woman is a figure of horror and pity. Think of Miss Havisham from Charles Dickens's *Great Expectations*, jilted at the altar in her youth and unable to move on, rustling pathetically through her crumbling mansion in a dusty, rotting wedding dress. That's the lonely lady patriarchy imagines, so fixated on her singleness that it dominates her life.

But when you have a solitary woman who's *not* obsessed with The Man (or Men) (or Other Love Interests) Who Got Away? That's when you get the crone.

As I head deeper into my crone years, I find myself craving more alone time. And it appears I have a lot of company. Maybe it's the caretaking role society assigns to us that results in our desire for solitude? Or our growing impatience with life's bullshit? Or the realization that time on this earth is ticking away? I believe that The Alone is where crones are made. Solitude is a safe harbor to find ourselves—or to return to the person we once were. Even the more super-social crones among us usually have some sort of solo practice: yoga, meditation, "me time." Whatever you call it, it's still The Alone. And it's our soulmate.

So don't fear The Alone, friends. Embrace it! Welcome it into your home. Give it a spot to sit and a mug of tea. Tell it your secrets, confide in it your fears. Open your whole self to it, and The Alone will be your North Star, guiding you toward cronedom.

Now, befriending The Alone doesn't necessarily mean *being* alone, at least not all the time. You're not required to break up with your partner or completely overhaul your life. You don't have to run away from home and embark on a two-thousand-mile solo road trip to make The Alone your BFF. (But if you do, some free advice: don't wait for the next gas station to pee. It may end badly.) It's just about taking the time and space to honor yourself.

So how exactly can we do that?

A ROOM OF ONE'S CRONE

Virginia Woolf wrote "a woman must have money and a room of her own if she is to write fiction." And while we're not technically writing fiction, we are outlining the story for the latter half of our life. This is the ideal time to check back in with your main character. (That's you.) What did she want in the past? What does she want now? Think about it: one way kids discover who they are is giving them the space to explore and play. So why wouldn't we need the same?

The first step to a room of one's own is finding your space. Few of us have the luxury of having a spare room to use in whatever witchy way we'd like. But you can carve out an area anywhere in the house: your bedroom, the bathroom, the weird nook in the hallway, the one corner of the basement that's colder than the rest of the room where a ghost probably lives.

Then, make that space your own—whatever that means for you. Maybe you fill it with houseplants or install your coziest blanket. Maybe you want to add your favorite smells with a candle or a fragrance stick diffuser. Take all your senses into account, and consider what makes you feel safe, comfortable, and welcome. But most of all, think about what makes a space feel like it belongs to *you.*

When my spouse and I bought our first house, the first thing I did was hang a painting of my pit bull, Daisy J. Dog (RIP), over the mantel. After my divorce, I moved back in with my parents . . . and the first thing I did was hang that same painting in my bedroom. While technically it was my childhood bedroom, it hadn't been my room for nearly thirty years. Everything about it was different now—including me. Hanging that painting of Daisy J. Dog (done by a friend of mine) made it feel like *my* space once again. And if I ever manage to move out (she wrote, sobbing), the painting of Daisy J. will be the first thing that goes up at my new place.

To make a space yours, figure out what makes a space *you.* What's your Daisy J. Dog painting? Obviously you're limited by the space you've carved out—crones with a home office will have more room than crones with half a shelf in the foyer. But you should be able to infuse your space with some kind of Essence of You. Some things to keep in mind:

* **It's not about achieving perfect crone vibes.** The goal isn't to style an area of your home to a certain aesthetic. You're not getting a two-page spread in *Better Crones and Gardens.*
* **It doesn't have to make sense.** In fact, being confused by the items you've gathered for your crone space can be a good thing! Maybe there's a part of you that you've lost or been ignoring, and your brain is trying to give you a gentle nudge.

* **You don't have to commit.** If you find the space isn't working for you, don't be afraid to reevaluate. You can swap items in and out at your whim. So don't be afraid to experiment.
* **Just make sure it speaks to you.** And nobody else's opinion matters.

We'll talk more about how to crone up your home decor in Chapter 3, but don't worry about thinking that big right now. You're not redecorating, you're just laying claim to a space where you can try to get in touch with your inner crone.

ALTAR-ED SPACE

Need more inspiration for claiming your space? Create an altar! In witchcraft, altars are spots for religious practice. But we're using *altar* very loosely here, as a reflection of your power and a place for performing any kind of personal rites or rituals. A classic altar based in Wicca or another witchcraft tradition might feature crystals, a magic wand or ceremonial dagger, an altar cloth, a chalice or ritual bowl, candles, religious figurines, and salt for protection or banishing. Your personal altar might instead include:

* A writing pen and journal, or art supplies
* Special jewelry, lucky objects, or mementos
* A favorite print or meaningful piece of art
* Your signature water bottle or wine goblet (I have a glass that reads BED WINE that is mine and everyone knows not to touch it!)
* Incense, plants, candles, or oils with a favorite or signature scent
* Snacks

A ROOM OF ONE'S OWN? IN THIS ECONOMY?

I dream of having a writing cabin in the woods to disappear to when I'm on deadline. (Or a fancy hotel with room service.) But space costs money, so "a room of one's own" is a privilege not every crone has.

So if you're a crone who doesn't have the space at home to be solo, take your act on the road. That means you'll have to bring your items with you, so they'll have to be more portable. If you're able, keep your items in a special bag (or box) that fits in your glove box (if you're a crone with a car) or purse. You can even get crafty and decorate your container so that it feels more personalized. Think of it like a traveling exhibit from the Museum of You.

Now's the tricky bit: finding a semipublic spot where you can be alone. Some ideas:

* Going for a long, meandering drive can cost a lot in gas . . . but going for a long, meandering walk is usually free. A solo walk with no destination is one of my favorite ways to get into—and out of—my head.
* However, if you have access to a car, park somewhere pretty. Just make sure that it's legal (and safe) to park. When I lived in Los Angeles, I would drive up to a vista on Mulholland Drive.
* Libraries aren't just for reading. They're a community hub providing necessary resources—like places to be alone. Your local branch probably has all sorts of cushy chairs, reading nooks, or study carrels. You might even find private study rooms to book for free. (Fun fact: I wrote most of this book in a corner of the library.)
* Belong to a gym? See if they'll let you sneak into the yoga room when it's not being used. (Or just do it. I won't tell.)
* If all else fails, noise-canceling headphones allow you to be alone anywhere: a public park, an airplane, your gynecologist's office. Slip them on, and magic! Instant alone time. (Just be aware of your surroundings, as some of them almost do too good a job at blocking out noise.)

Mad Madam Mim

Walt Disney's 1963 animated feature *The Sword in the Stone* follows the journey of a young King Arthur as he goes from an orphan mentored by Merlin himself to (spoiler alert) the King of England. But the real star of the show is Mad Madam Mim, the lavender-haired witch who lives alone in a cottage in the woods.

We meet Mim as she sits at her table playing a game of solitaire when Arthur (who's been transformed into a sparrow by Merlin) falls down her chimney. When bird-Arthur praises Merlin as the "world's most powerful wizard," Mim breaks into a song-and-dance number praising her own superior powers—"I'm the magnificent, marvelous Mad Madam Mim." Key to her magnificence: she can be whatever she wants to be (big, small, ugly, beautiful), and she delights in things others find gruesome. (Arthur still insists that Merlin's magic is more "useful" and "good," which is an experience that may be familiar to any crone— seeing her powerful sorcery immediately being written off by a twelve-year-old boy.)

Even if you don't share Mim's enjoyment of illness and decay, you've got to respect her enchantress chops—and her confidence. She's not quiet about the pride she takes in her knowledge and skill set. She's written a whole song about it! As an old woman, this makes her "crazy." As a man, it would make her a CEO.

Wising Up

The crone may be depicted as hideous, mean, and socially outcast, but even her detractors admit that she's full of wisdom. Wisdom is insight, judgment, and knowledge gained from life experience—it's not just something crones have naturally, but something they've earned by observing, making mistakes, recognizing patterns, and listening to other people. Don't confuse it with success, a meaningless metric defined by those in power. (If those guys had wisdom, we'd have affordable housing and fair pay instead of tax breaks and Cybertrucks.)

Have you ever heard your mother, aunt, or other female elder state an opinion and immediately follow it up with "but I don't know what I'm talking about"—even though they know exactly what they're talking about? That's how patriarchy wants us to regard our own wisdom—as tainted specifically because it comes from *our* experience, from *our* understanding.

A friend of mine volunteered for an organization supporting women with careers in science, technology, engineering, and math. She told me about a time she led a roundtable discussion with women and men about obstacles facing women in STEM. Every time a woman would describe her experience, a man would interrupt to agree: it was vital to listen to women! Then he would spend the next ten minutes describing all the times he personally witnessed men not listening to women.

That's what it feels like when people talk about the wisdom of crones. It's a compliment without any meaning, a man speaking over you to stress how important he thinks your voice is. Crones are supposed to be grateful to be given a chance to speak, but we shouldn't expect to be listened to.

This isn't limited to crones. All women frequently have their knowledge called into question—or explained back to them. A man once told me he was tired of the term *mansplaining*. I posited that the term would disappear when men stopped doing it. He proceeded to explain to me what mansplaining actually was, and how I had probably never even been mansplained to. This sort of response gets increasingly ridiculous and offensive the more wisdom you attain, but being gaslit about your lived experience and your personal expertise will be familiar to anyone who's been (or been seen as) a woman of any age.

So our wisdom is discounted, our knowledge is questioned, and our lived experience is second-guessed. No wonder our moms and our aunts and our grandmothers were always adding "but I don't know what I'm talking about" to the end of every sentence. What's a crone to do? Get in touch with our crone touchstones, obvi.

 SPELL IT OUT

Get in Touch with Your Touchstones

Our crone touchstones (**Wisdom**, **Knowledge**, and **Fuck It**) are the foundation of our crone ethos, and something we'll return to frequently in this book. The goal of this spell is to create literal touchstones to use as tangible, physical manifestations of your crone ideals. Think of them like a lucky charm or a favorite stuffed animal from your childhood.

YOU'LL NEED

* Three stones (representing **Wisdom**, **Knowledge**, and **Fuck It**)
* A bowl filled with water and a pinch of salt
* Art supplies for decorating your stones (optional)
* A windowsill or access to moonlight

THE RITUAL

* Place your stones into the salted water to work some cleansing magic. While the stones soak, gather your art supplies, if you're using them (it's also fine to leave your stones plain, or to choose your stones based on their natural aesthetics).

* When you feel the stones are ready, remove them from the water and dry them off. Decide which stone is going to represent each tenet.

* Clasp the stone in your hands (or tuck in your bra, or stuff it in your sock—you just want the stone to be touching your skin.) Close your eyes and take three deep breaths, centering yourself in this room, in this space, and in this moment. Then proceed depending on which stone you're working with.

* For your **Wisdom** stone, imagine a golden ball of light. This is all the wisdom in the universe. Now imagine that light flowing into you, traveling through your veins and straight to your heart. Feel the warmth from that glow and imagine it traveling from your heart, through your fingertips, and into the stone. This wisdom of the universe made personal by you. When you're ready, open your eyes and decorate your Wisdom stone (if you'd like).

* For your **Knowledge** stone, picture yourself in a library shaped like a circle—there are no corners, no edges, just an endless array of books. The books emanate a blue mist that buoys you, gently lifting you off the floor. As you ascend, you feel your synapses crackle to life, buzzing with knowledge. Feel the electricity travel through your brain, through your fingertips, and into your stone. When you're ready, open your eyes and decorate your Knowledge stone (if you'd like).

* For your **Fuck It** stone, imagine that you're floating in a sea of orange light that carries you to the place where you feel most free. Maybe it's floating in the Gulf of Mexico, or maybe it's feeding the crows in the

park, or maybe it's somewhere you haven't been but you dream of. The orange light infuses your entire body with a sense of joy, of freedom, of possibility. Send those vibrations from your body, through your fingertips, and into your stone. When you're ready, open your eyes and decorate your Fuck It stone (if you'd like).

* When you're finished, place all three stones on a windowsill (or outside if safe) to charge in the moonlight overnight. Behold: you've got touchstones!

THE PERSONAL GRIMOIRE

When I started therapy, I would jot down my thoughts after every session. Some may call it journaling. I preferred to think of it as creating my personal grimoire. A grimoire is a witch's handbook, a magical text containing spells, potions, charms, and enchantments. There may be instructions for how to create amulets or summon demons—and my ability to summon demons was why I was in therapy in the first place! I just needed some magic to learn how to live alongside the demons (or banish them altogether). If you find the idea of journaling corny or just haven't been able to get into it, perhaps you too will have an easier time if you think of it as compiling a personal grimoire.

Currently, I use my grimoire to record, well, everything. It's part feelings dump, part day planner, part recipe collection, part record of petty complaints, part compendium of random thoughts that I don't know where else to put. I find myself returning to my grimoire when I'm feeling lost. Flipping back through its pages, I see my journey with new eyes. There's some bit of wisdom from past me that suddenly makes sense to present me. Even if that wisdom is *stop worrying so damned much, you always figure it out.*

Many of you have spent your life thinking about other people. Your personal grimoire is a place to think just about yourself. It's a foundational tool for connecting to our crone touchstones, a reminder that you are filled with wisdom—even if the world tries to make you feel otherwise. It's also an excellent place to start musing on your crone superpowers.

Your Crone Superpowers

Crones, gather round in your hunchbacked, scraggly-haired, rheumy-eyed splendor. It's time to discuss that special time in every crone's life. I'm talking about the discovery of your powers.

Now, we can't avoid the fact that aging and loss go hand in hand. We lose parents, partners, friends. We lose bone density. For crones with uteruses, we lose our periods. We lose memories. We lose time. But there's a whole bunch of things we gain as we dive headfirst into our crone years. We gain the ability to exist in brand-new ways. Because now we can tap into a well of power that was previously inaccessible to us: our crone superpowers.

Fairy godmothers are always showing up at christenings to bestow their magical gifts on infant princesses. Which, honestly, seems like kind of a waste. What's a baby going to do with magic? At *best* they're learning shapes and colors; more likely they've only gotten as far as how to smile when they poop. And sure, sometimes fairy godmothers will show up past infancy to rustle up a pumpkin carriage, but once you reach cronehood? The fairy godmother disappears—taking her magical gifts with her.

That ends now. Your fairy godcrone has arrived! Along with your crone touchstones, I also bring a few new arrows to add to your magical quiver. So gather round, my friends. An array of mystical talents awaits!

I DON'T GIVE A FLYING FUCK

The power of I Don't Give a Flying Fuck, also sometimes known as Barren Field of Fucks or simply Fucklessness, is your complete lack of concern for what anyone thinks about who you are, what you look like, or what you do. This power stems from our third touchstone (**Fuck It**, to do what we please) and is often the first power to make itself known to the crone. It can reveal itself bit by bit or all at once. I bet you've already put it into action at least once, but here are some additional ways it can be used.

BEHOLD! THE POWER TO:

* **Look ridiculous:** Wear what you want, how you want, when you want. Arrange your body in whatever way makes you most comfortable. Dye your hair blue. Pierce your nose. Get a tattoo. Wear a stuffed parrot on your shoulder and call her Sparky. (I knew someone who did this. Crone goals!) Clashing patterns, purple lipstick, indulging every style whim you've ever had. What would have gotten you eye-rolled out of the conference room when you were still trying to impress people will now probably earn you the titles of *brave* and *an icon*.

* **Let that fury flag fly:** Do you find yourself speaking out more and shutting up less? Congrats! You've just leveled up. You are not "fine." You are tired. You are furious. And you are done. If the patriarchy is such a fan of shutting up, maybe they should try it sometime!

* **Eat food:** I don't know about you, but I spent my first forty years on this planet denying myself food. I didn't eat in front of my first boyfriend for nearly a year. A year. I'm sure I'm not the only one: diet culture and Western beauty standards did a number on a lot of us. Your appetite is your friend. Feed it.

When people are asked "what's the superpower you'd want most?" the top answer is invisibility. And guess what, crones? We're invisible! However, when it comes to women of a certain age, *invisible* is usually described as a bad thing. Hell, I described it that way earlier in this chapter. How can being unseen be a benefit? No one wants to be overlooked or ignored! But we can't choose what superpowers are bestowed upon us. So no need to get angry or depressed. Being invisible is a place where your crone wisdom and knowledge can really shine. Here are just a few ways to use your powers of invisibility to your advantage.

BEHOLD! THE POWER TO:

* **Bypass the haters:** Going unseen comes in handy when it comes to encountering people with clipboards in the Trader Joe's parking lot or your conservative neighbor at the gym. If they sense your haunted wraith energy and perceive you in any way, simply ignore them. You can blame it on your aging brain if they ever mention it!

* **Bang the drum all day:** Making judgments about women's sex lives is the patriarchy's favorite pastime. But it's difficult to judge something that you can't (or refuse to) see. Use the Cloak of Unfuckability to indulge in your deepest desires. Intrigued by kink? Interested in spouse-swapping? Bi-curious? As long as it's safe and consensual, go out and play.

* **See into their souls:** It's shocking what folks will say or do when they don't clock your presence. Whether it's an embarrassing admission, vile behavior, or just hot goss, the crone witnesses it all!

* **Haunt all the places:** I stopped writing in public in my late twenties because every time I opened up my laptop, some guy wanted to quiz me about my work. Now I can sit uninterrupted for hours, typing away like the imperceptible specter I was meant to be!

A certain subset of crones—white (or white passing), cis (or cis passing)—have an additional power called Speaking to the Manager. This could also be called Karening for Good. (Or simply Privilege.) Speaking to the Manager is when you poke your crooked, warty nose into situations where it absolutely is called for, even if it might not be welcome—like calling attention to an issue or escalating a complaint. Most people won't harm a crone, and whiteness and cisness afford extra protection. (*Most* is doing heavy lifting here. Be safe out there!)

Speaking to the Manager utilizes all three of your crone touchstones: your **Wisdom** to recognize what's right, your **Knowledge** of when and how to intervene, your **Fuck It** to say what needs to be said. But this power should always be used *for* people, not *at* them. Your good intent could have a terrible impact, ending up harming people you intended to help. So it's always a good idea to ask if they want your help first!

BEHOLD! THE POWER TO:

* **Call out microaggressions:** If being direct makes you nervous, look confused and ask the person what they mean. Watch them flop-sweat as they try to explain why their racist joke was funny.
* **Provide cover:** This can be used for intense situations, like trying to organize a tenant union or standing up to the boss. But it can also apply to mentorship. I worked with a young Mexican artist to develop an idea of hers into an animated show—the creative work came from her, but because I have more experience, I was able to shield her from common errors, give her a boost over potholes, and offer support and advice when she hit obstacles. Providing cover meant sharing my skills and getting out of her way. (And hopefully one day she can do the same for a less experienced creator!)

* **De-escalate:** De-escalation is a specific process used to calm a conflict. You're not saving the day—you're just bringing the temperature down. The nonthreatening nature of crones makes them uniquely suited for this role. But this can be dangerous, so you can't just wing it. If you're interested in learning more, look up "bystander intervention" or "conflict de-escalation" online for tips and classes in your area.

* **Apologize:** The power of a genuine apology cannot be overstated. But this power may need some work on our part. So your apology should not be an "I'm sorry, but . . ." or "I'm sorry you feel that way." An apology should include not only "sorry" but also what you're apologizing for—and the steps you're taking to correct it.

These are just a few of your crone superpowers—you may discover more. And you didn't even have to be bitten by a radioactive spider, subjected to a secret government experiment, or be the daughter of Zeus. But you did have to become a crone, and to be honest? That's more than enough work.

Marie Laveau

You may know Marie Laveau as a character on *American Horror Story* played by real-life goddess Angela Bassett. But Marie Laveau was an actual person. Born a free Black woman in Louisiana in 1801, Laveau was a crone virtuoso. She did it all: Voodoo practitioner. Prison reformer. Midwife. Clairvoyant. Hairdresser.

Laveau was known as the Voodoo Queen of New Orleans, publicly practicing the religion of the African diaspora even though it was outlawed in the territory. (She was also a practicing Catholic, and it's said that this helped shield her from the powers that be.)

Community was at the heart of Marie Laveau's life. Her prison ministry saw her seeking leniency for prisoners sentenced to death and praying with those whose condemnation was imminent. She posted bond for Black women accused of petty crimes. She cared for victims of cholera, fed the poor, and even sponsored educations for orphans.

How did Laveau fund her charitable works? Through her beauty parlor.

While our queen was the go-to hairdresser for the New Orleans upper class, she wasn't just using her skills for setting curls. Her salon was filled with rich white women who loved to gossip. So Laveau would listen in, filing the juicy tidbits away. Later, when the same women would engage her services as a clairvoyant, Laveau would repackage these tidbits as insights. The women were none the wiser—but Laveau was quite the richer.

When she died, her death was reported in papers across the country. She was described as "a woman of great beauty, intellect, and charisma who was also pious, charitable, and a skilled herbal healer."

Marie Laveau: the Queen of Voodoo—and of crones.

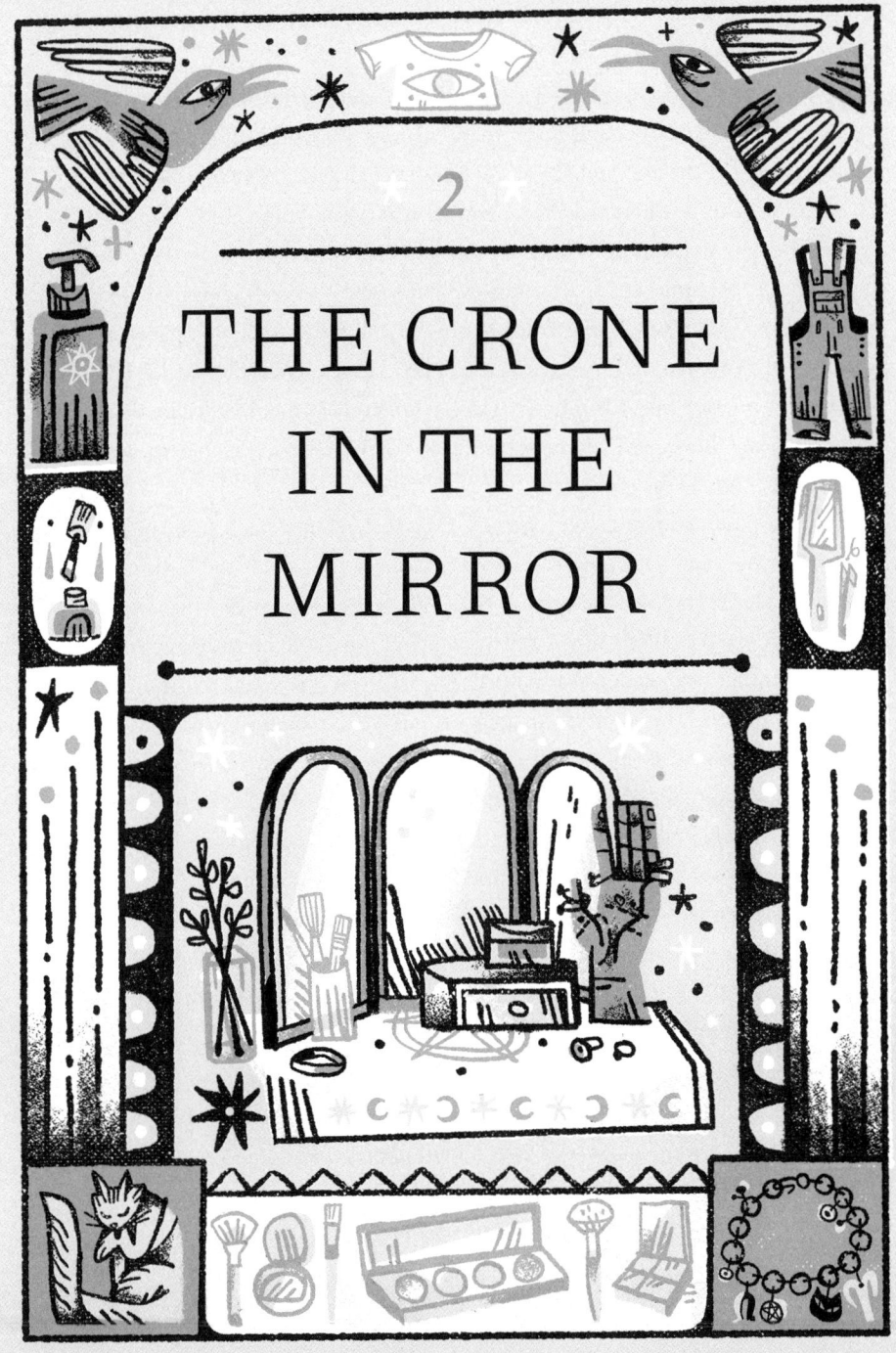

2

THE CRONE
IN THE
MIRROR

It's the early 1980s. I'm in a wide, open room with bright lights and gold-flecked carpet and floor-to-ceiling mirrors. The faint scent of Shalimar hangs in the air. And I'm at the most exclusive club I've ever been to in my nine years on this earth: the Loehmann's communal dressing room.

The room buzzes with older women with streaks of white in their hair, wearing the same shade of coral-pink lipstick and in various stages of undress. Chic outfits hang from hooks on the wall: cocktail dresses and lounging pajamas (!!!), caftans and jeweled tunics. It's a blur of fabric as they try on each one. My mother is also trying on clothes, but decidedly less fancy. She's the second-youngest person in the room by at least twenty years. (I am, of course, the youngest.)

While the women aren't together, they still act as a pack, assisting one another into and out of outfits. After the zippers are zipped and buttons are buttoned, the tryer-on studies her reflection in the mirror. She turns to the Greek chorus of older women and asks: "Am I too old to be wearing this?"

The other women don't say a word. The tryer-on turns back to the mirror. She comments how her arms are getting floppy, holding one up and flicking it to show how her skin wobbles. "I don't have crow's feet, I have the whole damn leg!" another one remarks. A third woman joins in: "At least your tits are above your navel!" These are the most glamorous women I have ever seen. They look like they ride around in chauffeured cars and solve crimes with dogs named Asta. But all they see is that they are getting old.

Loehmann's is now closed and gone (RIP), as are those women, I would imagine. (RIP.) But what's not gone is the societal expectation that women should apologize for their aging bodies and faces. If we embrace our older selves, we're shriveled-up hags. If we plump up our wrinkles and cover our grays, we're pathetic or trying too hard. It's a game that's impossible to win. Which is why the crone is wise enough not to play.

In the previous chapter, we learned about how to contact our inner crone. Now it's time to show the world what that bad witch looks like. Our crone era is about saying *fuck it* and committing to our purest selves. We'll banish what no longer serves us, so that we can embrace what does. No longer will we throw ourselves on the pyre of aging, wailing AM I TOO OLD FOR THIS? into the dark, starry night. We'll use the pyre to burn it all down. So run a brush through your stringy white hair, pull on that tattered black cloak, powder that warty nose, and grab your broomsticks, friends. Now's the time to let your crone aesthetic shine!

IN THIS CHAPTER, WE'LL LEARN:

* How to develop your signature crone style
* How to confront your closet
* Why the caftan is the crone's best friend
* What to do with your gray hair (if you want to do anything at all)
* How to face your aging face

Color Me Crone

If you're a Gen X crone like me, you may remember a certain cursed spellbook that epitomizes the 1980s and early '90s. That book was *Color Me Beautiful*, a grim tome that categorized women into seasons—winter, spring, summer or autumn—according to their hair, eye, and skin color. Forget being a Leo or a Capricorn—were you a winter or a spring? Whatever season you were assigned dictated the colors you looked best in.

My mom didn't own the book, but she did one step better. When I was in seventh grade, she paid for me to get my colors done. I sat at the kitchen table of a strange woman who held up swatches of fabric to my face to explain that I was a winter, which meant I looked best in black, white, red, or jewel tones. She also suggested that I use a lavender-tinted cream to "balance" my olive skin and make it "less green." (I may be only 99 percent Eastern European, but I'm 100 percent witch.)

But while I passed on the lavender-tinted cream, *Color Me Beautiful* clearly cast some sort of glamour on me. Even as a grown-ass crone, I still dress like a winter. (It's mostly black. But still.)

So while the haunted time capsule *Color Me Beautiful* may be a spiritual predecessor to Color Me Crone, I like to think of our color system more like Athena springing from Zeus's forehead, fully formed. The category you fall into isn't determined by a "warm" or "cool" skin tone—it's determined by your vibe, and you get to choose the one that feels right to you. (We are no longer letting our style be dictated by Some Lady!) It's pure aesthetic: four kinds of crones paired with four classic elements to create a ready-to-wear style guide. And what the hell, we'll throw in seasons, too.

WOODS CRONE

Element: Fire

Season: Autumn

Colors: Deep reds, burnt orange, mustard yellow

Color inspiration: The changing leaves

Style vibe: The quintessential tea-drinking, dusty-library-owning, mice-befriending witch. Think cozy, layered garments made of natural fibers: long skirts, chunky sweaters, fingerless gloves, long knit scarves that smell like woodsmoke. Clothing is tailored but not tight: ideal for rolling out pie dough or putting up the garden's last produce, all in preparation for a long winter's nap.

BEACH CRONE

Element: Water

Season: Summer

Colors: Blues, greens, and every combination in between

Color inspiration: The ocean

Style vibe: A crone who knows how to make a splash. This witch looks like she's always on vacation: flowing caftans and cover-ups, bikinis or one-piece swimsuits, and palazzo pants. Every outfit is covered in playful patterns, with slides to match. Sunglasses always make a statement—oversized, heart-shaped, or cat-eyed. Smells vaguely like coconut, but whether it's due to her lip gloss or her piña colada is anyone's guess.

ARCTIC CRONE

Element: Air

Season: Winter

Colors: White, silver, black

Color inspiration: The knowable and unknowable void

Style vibe: Often mistaken for an ice queen, but probably just over it. Clothing is simple—think leggings, turtlenecks, and boots year-round—and tends toward a single color. Can't resist a statement piece of jewelry. Clothing is snug, not bulky, allowing ease of movement. Smells your fear.

GARDEN CRONE

Element: Earth

Season: Spring

Colors: Greens, browns, bright oranges and yellows

Color inspiration: The first flowers of the growing season

Style vibe: Part earth mother, part mad scientist, this witch is always on the go—building, planting, planning, or creating. Clothing tends to be practical or activity-focused—think ripped jeans, athleisure, a long skirt paired with a tee and spotless sneakers. Patterns are playful but never loud. Smells faintly of dark, loamy soil.

Of course, one of the beauties of cronehood is that you never have to limit yourself to only the options that are in front of you. Embody one of these crone archetypes that speaks to you, or mix and match—choose a different one every day, or assemble your own style season.

The Crone Closet

Like a lot of us, I have a complicated history with my body. It would be easy to blame that history on the common culprits: the media, society, patriarchy. And trust me, I do! But my issues go a little deeper than that.

Due to the genetic cards I was dealt, I was, as my mom puts it, "the only six-year-old with hips." In third grade, I skipped the training bra and went straight for the pros. By the time I reached middle school, I wore a bigger cup size than most of my teachers. It was like my body was jealous that my brain was in the gifted program and wanted a piece of the action. I remember feeling annoyed that my rapidly developing body made playing sports (baseball and basketball) more difficult. But . . . I didn't feel bad about my body. I didn't hate it.

What I hated was how everyone else reacted to it. I hated that there were few tween clothes that fit me, and those that did got me called a slut. I hated that grown men catcalled me from their cars. I hated that male classmates made snide comments under their breath and tried to grope me in the hallways and during class. I hated that when I complained or sought help, I was told to be better, act nicer, dress differently. That, basically, everyone else's reaction to my body was my fault, and it was up to me to fix it.

(Yes, those adults sucked. As for those boys, well, I don't say their names like Arya Stark before I fall asleep each night. But like Pepperidge Farm, a crone remembers.)

It's not the sort of mantle you should place on an eleven-year-old's shoulders. But I didn't exactly have a choice. So I learned to harness the power of my clothing: to use it as armor, to wield it as a weapon, and to project the image of myself that I wanted to be. Over time, this developed into my own sense of style—a style that has carried into cronedom.

Now, your relationship with clothing may not be that deep. (Hopefully it isn't.) But look upon your crone era as an opportunity to experiment. Invite your **Fuck It** into the dressing room and reinvent yourself sartorially. Or use your years of **Wisdom** and **Knowledge** to lean into the image of the crone you want to be. Whether you're looking for a little style sorcery or a full magical makeover, it's time to contemplate the crone closet!

OWN YOUR STYLE

A decade ago, I purchased a long-sleeved fuzzy rainbow-striped sweater. I loved the way it looked on me, and everyone was always telling me that I should add some color to my wardrobe. In my closet, the sweater looked like an interloper swimming in a sea of black and gray. Every meeting, every hangout, every date, I'd vow to free the sweater from closet captivity. But it never saw the light of day, or even the chill of night. It sat there, year after year, a rainbow that never stretched farther than the threshold of my closet door. No longer able to take the sweater's almost mocking cheeriness, I set it free. (I gave it to a friend. It's her problem now.)

While I'm a proud bisexual, rainbow-colored clothing has rarely found a place in my wardrobe. I'm a goth! I knew that when I bought the sweater, but I thought I could find a way to make it work. To shove that round, rainbow peg into the inky-black, void-shaped hole. What I realized is that not giving a fuck isn't always about taking style chances and expanding our horizons.

It's about doing what we please. I liked the *idea* of being the kind of person who wears a fuzzy rainbow sweater. (Sort of how I like the idea of being the kind of person who "likes hiking.") I felt like I should expand my wardrobe to involve a color that wasn't associated with the depths of despair. But it turns out that despair is my natural uniform.

In other words, we are no longer using personal style to convey who we wish we were, who we think we might be someday, or who we want to fool other people (or ourselves) into thinking we are. In your crone era, personal style is for one thing only: being yourself, no matter what other people think of it. But often we've spent so long dressing to hide or change ourselves that we don't know how to dress when we want to highlight ourselves. At those times, you might need to check in with your crone touchstones and figure out what your style really is.

So whether you're a crone who wants to experiment with a new look or you're a crone like me who wants to conjure her stylish daily costume as quickly as possible, the following activity will cast a cohesion spell on your entire wardrobe—and avoid the curse of the lone rainbow sweater.

STYLE MAD LIBS

You remember Mad Libs—the word game that was a staple of sleepovers. You'd be asked for adjectives and nouns and verbs and adverbs, which would be used to fill in the blanks of a story. The final product would be read aloud to peals of laughter. It was oddly wholesome, even when we filled in the blanks with every swear word we knew.

Instead of crafting a silly story, we're crafting our crone look. Using an array of nouns and adjectives, we'll get to the heart of our crone style. Whether a winter coat or sweatpants, a summer shift or a basic tee, use Style Mad Libs as a technique to guide your crone style. And while Mad Libs usually has you coming up with words to fill in the blanks, here's a few suggestions to jump start your style journey.

ADJECTIVES	NOUNS
⬦ Dreamy	⬦ Swamp
⬦ Evil	⬦ Biker
⬦ Retro	⬦ Goblin
⬦ Preppy	⬦ Hag
⬦ Androgynous	⬦ Goth
⬦ Sporty	⬦ Witch
⬦ Scary	⬦ Unicorn
⬦ Posh	⬦ Ballerina
⬦ Medieval	⬦ Granny
⬦ Ethereal	⬦ Mermaid
⬦ Mysterious	⬦ Fairy
⬦ Futuristic	⬦ Librarian
⬦ Beachy	⬦ Exec
⬦ Anime	⬦ Alien
⬦ Metal	⬦ Astronaut
⬦ Art Deco	⬦ Supervillain
⬦ Goth	⬦ Cryptid
⬦ Granola	⬦ Babe
⬦ Business	⬦ Warrior
⬦ Boho	⬦ Void

Mix and match to your heart's content. Preppy granny? Art Deco mermaid? Sporty goth? Goth exec? If none of these options call out to you, check out style blogs, fashion magazines, or even a thesaurus to choose words that resonate. (They don't have to be style terms, either—maybe you find *invertebrate* inspiring in a way *normcore* could never be.)

Once you've landed on your look, anytime you're considering a purchase (or cleaning out your closet), ask yourself one simple question: *Does this fit my newly defined aesthetic?* For example, my style guide is *supervillain.* So when pondering a purchase, I ask: Would a supervillain wear that?

The end result is a wardrobe consisting mostly of black and gray clothes, with the occasional leopard print thrown in. (Leopard print is a neutral, I will die on this hill.) My everyday uniform is a casual black dress (and boots), or jeans and a black top (and boots). My dressier clothes are more body-conscious or form-fitting—fancier (black) dresses, (black) wiggle skirts, (black) turtlenecks. Imagine *Mad Men*'s Joan Holloway clad in a business-appropriate catsuit, crushing the bosses of Sterling Cooper under her shiny black boot heel. Nary a stray fuzzy rainbow sweater to be found!

CHOOSE YOUR FIGHTER!

Our clothes protect us from the world. They keep us insulated from the elements, but I didn't do a deep dive into my adolescent nightmare to explain how to prevent your nipples from getting frostbite. When I talk about clothes as armor, I'm talking about how our clothes make us feel—and how we can use them to manipulate how people see us.

A perfect example of clothing as armor? The iconic '80s power suit, a staple in every chic corporate raider's closet. The source of the power suit's power was contained in its shoulder pads. The pads jutted out, cutting a wide and imposing figure: a ruthless inverted triangle ready to bust unions and plunder employee retirement accounts.

But your armor doesn't have to be aggressively confrontational. It can be a warning to back off. Or it can be a cloak of protection, rendering you completely unperceived, a wraith haunting the produce section of the supermarket. Here are some style-as-armor suggestions for everyone from the power suits to the power bottoms!

PLATE ARMOR
When you want to feel untouchable, go for clothing that's physically protective.

* Motorcycle jackets
* Spikes
* Chain mail accessories
* Head-to-toe leather

DAZZLE ARMOR
Are you willing to be perceived, but you want to be perceived as confusing and perhaps even dangerous? Take a page from nature (specifically, poison frogs).

* Clashing patterns
* Leopard print catsuits
* Neon leotards
* Clown pants
* Fright wigs

BOUNDARY ARMOR
When you want to feel cute—but you also want to keep people at arm's length.

* Hoop skirts
* Bridesmaids gowns (specifically '80s ones with giant sleeves and bows)

* Huge shoulder pads
* Even longer spikes

ORGANIC ARMOR

When you're looking for something naturally repellant!

* Ratty sweatsuit
* IRS field office jacket
* Clipboard and badge (accessories more than clothing, but these will keep people far away, especially in grocery store parking lots)

CONFRONTING YOUR CLOSET

Our crone era is about committing to our purest selves, banishing what no longer serves us and embracing what does. So it's time to take what we've discovered about our signature crone style and put that magic to work. Time to take stock of our stock. It's time to confront our closets. (And dressers. And wardrobes. And bedroom floors. Wherever you're keeping your clothes.)

I know, I know. Cleaning out the closet can be the worst. Clothes are a visual catalog of our life, so going through them can feel like a trip down memory lane—if memory lane was in a carnival funhouse. Mine feels like just a whole bunch of distorted images, haunting my dreams: the expensive designer jeans that fit for seven minutes in summer 2006. The sparkly silver platform boots that I was wearing the night I got roofied. My favorite black dress wadded up in a ball, a victim of my inability to take anything to the dry cleaners. That rainbow sweater, reminding me that even as a grown-ass woman, I have no idea how to shop for myself.

However, it's not all regret and failure. You'll probably unearth some buried gems. I thought my magical black shirtdress that fits at every size and is incapable of wrinkling was lost to the ages. Nope, just hanging on for dear life to some out-of-the-way hanger. My mother's vintage necklace that she gifted me a decade ago was languishing on a shelf. The perfect pair of goth-spiked business casual loafers were buried in my closet because they had gone unworn for so long. (Zoom meetings mean no loafers required.)

Think of cleaning out your closet like a purification spell, freeing up physical and mental space. Your dresser drawers will no longer be jam-packed. You'll be able to see the clothes in your closet. You'll release the past that no longer serves you (goodbye, patent leather stilettos! Farewell, tailored pantsuit!) so that you can embrace what the present—and future—has in store.

> Cleaning out your closet doesn't mean you should buy all new stuff—especially not fast fashion! Consumer clothing waste is wreaking havoc on the environment and disproportionately affects countries in the Global South. For more information, check out Aja Barber's book *Consumed: The Need for Collective Change: Colonialism, Climate Change, and Consumerism.*

Start in the bedroom (or wherever you keep your clothes.) Go through your clothing, piece by piece, and ask your crone style question:

1. Would a [*your crone style*] wear this?
* **Yes:** Fold, hang, or place in a pile to be put away at the end.
* **No:** Go to the next step.

2. Can I repurpose this to make it work for me?
* **Yes:** Can a panel be added to a bodice to create more room? Can a dress be transformed into a skirt? Can two shirts be combined to create a *clashing pattern megashirt*? Set it aside to be repurposed.
* **No:** Go to the next step.

3. Is this in good enough condition to be donated (or sold)?
* **Yes:** Put it in a pile for donation.
* **No:** Put in a pile for recycling.

4. Put away the clothing you're going to repurpose or keep, then proceed to the Purify Your Closet spell.

SPELL IT OUT

:* Purify Your Closet ⋆⁺

We've got two spells for two sets of clothing: items to be donated (or sold, if that's your jam), and items to be recycled.

THE WASTEFUL BRACELET

This spell is to encourage us to be mindful when it comes to our clothing purchases. It won't magically break the curse of fast fashion or clothing waste, but maybe it'll leave a dent.

YOU'LL NEED

* Your clothing to be recycled
* A big bag
* Scissors

THE RITUAL

1. Sort through your recycling pile and select one item of clothing that was truly a waste (like an item bought for a costume and never worn again).
2. Place the rest of the items in your recycling bag.

3. Use scissors to cut the waste item into strips of fabric.

4. Create a fabric bracelet out of the strips by braiding, tying, or knotting the pieces together. This is your wasteful bracelet!

5. The next time you're mulling over any potential clothing purchase, slip on your bracelet and ask yourself: *Will this become the next wasteful bracelet?*

BLESS AND BANISH!

Now that we've addressed our clothing waste, it's time to attack the donation pile!

YOU'LL NEED

* Your clothing to be donated

* A bag

THE RITUAL

1. Make a circle with the clothes from your donation pile.

2. Pick up an item of clothing and decide if it's a bless or banish.
   - **Banish:** Clothing that haunts you (my rainbow sweater!)
   - **Bless:** Clothing that you love but are ready to say goodbye to, clothing you hold no ill will toward

3. Bid the item farewell. Get as personal or profane as you'd like.
   - **Banish:** "Pants, begone! Into the void where you belong!" "Fuck off into the sea, these jeans mean nothing to me!"
   - **Bless:** "Many blessings to this blouse, it's time to find a new house."

4. Place the item in the bag. Repeat until the donate pile is gone.

Enter the Caftan

The classic crone haunts the liminal space between the real world and the magical one. Part of her odd allure is her tattered cloak. The well-worn garment obscures her shape, making her appear styleless and shabby. But the crone's tattered cloak is also enigmatic. One can't help but wonder about what hides beneath the folds of threadbare fabric. What magic does it contain? What curiosities does it conceal? It kinda makes you want a tattered cloak of your own.

Enter the caftan.

The caftan (or kaftan) dates back to ancient Mesopotamia (what's known now as Iraq, Syria, and Turkey), where the loose-fitting, ornate silk or cotton robes were worn mostly by men. But after Diana Vreeland sang the caftan's praises in the pages of *Vogue* in the 1960s, the caftan boom was born. Caftans could be found on the runways of designers such as Emilio Pucci, Halston, Thea Porter, and Yves Saint Laurent. But caftans were also adopted by the counterculture, worn by hippies and musicians alike. Then they just seemed to disappear from everyone's fashion landscape. Everyone *except* older women.

The caftan is *the* foundational garment of the crone starter pack. We should get a coupon for one with our AARP card. Why? Oh, I was hoping you'd ask.

* **The caftan always fits.** It doesn't care if you're bloated. Or your weight fluctuates. Or you're just feeling weird in your body. The caftan's got your back.
* **The caftan is cool.** Hot flashes? Night sweats? Climate change? The caftan's flowy fabric keeps the air circulating around your body, so even swamp witches feel less swampy.
* **The caftan is simple.** There's no zippers to break, belts to lose, or bits and bobs to get caught on things.

* **The caftan is comfy.** It's like wearing your nightgown in public—except you could show up at an awards ceremony and nobody would bat an eye.
* **The caftan lends an aura of mystery and glamour.** Whether it's fashionable or frumpy, every caftan adds a certain je ne sais quoi to its wearer. Kind of like . . . magic.

The caftan is the chic version of the crone's tattered cloak. In fact, there are some ways the caftan is—dare I say—even better?

CAFTAN VS. CLOAK

Tattered cloak: Heavy, dusty, takes ages to achieve that perfectly tattered look.
Caftan: Ready to wear!

Tattered cloak: Screams "I am here to curse your child."
Caftan: Goes from pool to party—you'll blend in so well that you'll be able to curse twice the babies in half the time!

Tattered cloak: Vintage ones smell like dampness and decay.
Caftan: Vintage ones smell like Chanel No. 5 and Newports!

Tattered cloak: Has pockets
Caftan: Also can have pockets!

You can buy caftans brand-new, but I recommend looking at vintage stores or resale shops. Crones who sew can make their own, or you can commission them from someone else. During the pandemic, I bought a few handmade caftans on Etsy—some sellers will even let you choose your own fabric.

LET'S GET DRESSED!

Don't know how to style your caftan? Witch, I got you.

The casual caftan: For the crone on the go

* Perfect for apothecary errands or running out to the magical market
* Look for caftans made of cotton or linen blends.
* Pair with sneakers or comfy slides, and finish the look with oversized sunglasses and a tote bag.

The formal caftan: For the crone on the town

* Perfect for all your enchanted evenings, galas, and balls
* Look for caftans made of gauze, georgette, silk, or challis—or sequins.
* Pair with metallic flats, strappy sandals, or shiny booties. Finish with red lipstick and bejeweled statement jewelry—think brooches, necklaces, bracelets, even a small crown.

The conjuring caftan: For the crone doing serious magic

* Perfect for all your midnight meetings and blood moon rituals
* Look for caftans made of fabric that speaks to you. Literally.
* Pair with cursed amulets, silk scarves (for spell casting or keeping your hair out of your face), and comfortable shoes. The trek back to the car after a late-night new moon ceremony is always longer than you think!

Endora

Samantha Stephens: That was a mean,
low, sneaky, underhanded trick!

Endora: Yes, it was.
And I'm quite pleased with myself.

Endora was suburban witch Samantha's mom on the 1960s and '70s sitcom *Bewitched* (which you probably saw on Nick at Nite). Played by Agnes Moorehead—whose acting career spanned five decades—she was not only a powerful witch but a meddling mother-in-law, doting grandma, and style icon.

Witch wife Samantha Stephens just wanted to conform to suburban life with her human husband, Darrin. But Endora was having none of that. She was an opinionated crone who refused to blend in. Looking like a mash-up of Auntie Mame and Baby Jane, Endora would appear out of nowhere cloaked in colorful caftans, clunky jewelry, and her signature blue eye shadow and black winged eyeliner.

Because Endora is a different kind of crone. You won't find her living in a dusty cottage in the woods. She'd have a condo in a desert senior community, where she'd teach classes on tantric sex and have a much younger boyfriend. She's the Palm Springs prophesier of our dreams. Sure, she could be hard on Samantha's husband, her son-in-law Darrin. But that's just part of her charm. (And he probably deserved it.)

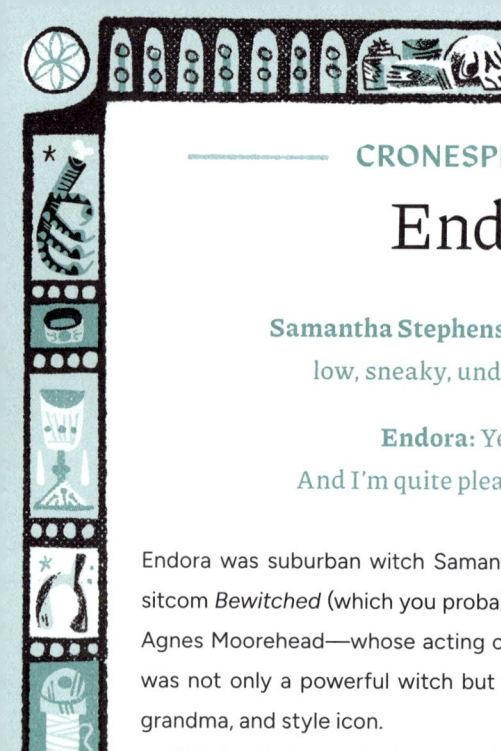

The Age-Old Question

This chapter began in the early 1980s in the Loehmann's communal dressing room with a crowd of women in their fifties and sixties asking: *Am I too old to be wearing this?* The answer back then was no. And the answer today is still no. The idea that we're too old to wear something is ridiculous. It's a cultural cudgel used in an attempt to somehow put us in our place. But our place is much like our style: it's whatever the hell we want.

I may not be able to prevent society from asking *aren't you too old to wear that?* But hopefully I can get you to stop asking yourself that question, and all the other questions that fall under its umbrella: *Is this skirt too short? Is this red lipstick too much? Is this V-neck too low-cut? Do I have the right to bare arms?* They're all reworked versions of the same boring question.

Now, if you're someone who has always asked yourself those questions, who's always been hypercritical of your appearance and what is and isn't "acceptable"? Cronedom won't automatically change that—at least not at first.

But pay attention to how the world treats you as you enter your crone era. Pay attention to how the world treats other crones. Because that's the first step to finding your **Fuck It**. And *fuck it* is the answer to this question.

Is this skirt too short? *Fuck it.* Is this red lipstick too much? *Fuck it.* Is this V-neck too low-cut? *Fuck it.* Do I have the right to bare arms? *Fuck it.*

Am I too old to be wearing this? *Fuck it.*

Gray Area(s)

If I've learned anything from the refrigerator magnets sold at my local drugstore, kids are the number-one cause of gray hairs. (And empty wallets, according to the same magnet.) Refrigerator magnet wisdom aside, gray hair is blamed on everything from stress and anxiety to electromagnetic frequencies and gut microbiomes.

But the reality is a tad more boring. The age you start going gray is, like most things, dictated by genetics. Which is annoying (you have zero control over it) but also freeing (you have zero control over it!). My baba—who escaped both Stalin and Hitler with her husband, a toddler, and a mother-in-law who hated her in tow—started really going gray in her sixties. The only things I've ever escaped were a couple of bad relationships and being recruited into LuLaRoe, and yet I started going gray in my forties. Whenever it shows up, though, gray (or white) hair is a follicular harbinger: cronedom is coming.

There's already so much societal messaging about our hair: Long hair is feminine, extremely short hair is not. Mothers are encouraged to cut their hair to make "one less thing to worry about" after having kids. Black women carry the additional burden of having their natural hair criticized, politicized, and penalized.

We're taught to fear gray hair because gray hair means we're getting old. And if we don't cover our grays, we'll look old. And if we look old, then people will know we're old. So it's never been about what gray hair looks like, because it looks cool as hell. It's about what it represents. And gray hair signals to the world that we're aging. Once again, we're penalized for the crime of continuing to have a birthday.

So what's a crone to do? Do you embrace your new follicular overlords? Do you wrestle your grays into submission with hair dye? Do you tap out and shave it off entirely? These are all excellent questions that I won't personally be able to answer for you. But you know what can? Our crone touchstones.

Wisdom, to know who we are

Knowledge, to understand what we want

Fuck It, to do what we please

You can use the touchstones to get to the root (get it?) of how you feel about your hair—whether that's about covering your gray or something more drastic. (Mohawk, anyone?)

Wisdom: Is this something you even care about? Is hair important to your self-concept?

Knowledge: What does your ideal hair look like? How much time or money or patience will it require?

Fuck It: Are there outside influences standing in the way of your hair choices? Think peer pressure, societal messaging, career issues, and the like. What would it take for you to get past them?

I mentioned going gray in my forties—but I don't have gray hair. I have blue hair. I've had blue hair for almost a decade. Growing up, I wasn't allowed to make decisions about my hair—my mom decided I was getting a perm, end of discussion. (Gen X crones know what I'm talking about.) Throughout my twenties and thirties, I vacillated between various shades of red and black and dark purple. I had wanted to dye it blue, but I was always told blue was the most difficult color to keep up. When I voiced this to my new hairdresser, she scoffed. Blue? No problem. She dyed my hair blue. And it's been varying shades of blue ever since. So here's how that journey through the touchstones looked for me:

Wisdom: I am, and always have been, a person who wants to have a weird color of hair. That's important to me and I'm willing to put up with a certain amount of effort and expense to achieve it. And I've wanted my hair to be blue since I was a little girl and discovered that hair dye was even a thing.

Knowledge: Getting my hair professionally dyed isn't cheap and it takes hours every time. I'm not supposed to take hot showers or shampoo too often. That's what it takes to achieve my vision of blue hair, and it's worth it to me.

Fuck It: There aren't any professional norms for me to worry about when it comes to work. Blue hair doesn't just make me more memorable to execs and companies that might hire me, it's considered "fun"—a plus when you write kids' TV (which I often do.) Nothing to overcome there! My stylist did mention that strangers (mostly men) always talked to her more when she had blue hair, but I've got strategies for dealing with that (I usually acknowledge the compliment because it's just easier and I have a life to live). And if anyone else has an opinion—fuck it!

My blue hair isn't intended to fool anyone into thinking I'm younger—although I'm aware that it often does. That's not my reason for dyeing it (my reason is: I want blue hair and I can't grow it that way myself). However, it's completely cool and understandable if you're a crone who would like to embrace her gray hair but doesn't because you're worried about ageism. Sometimes you have the wisdom and knowledge to realize you're not ready to say *fuck it*, and that's fine too.

Facing Your Face

It's 2019 and I'm sitting in my hairstylist's chair, waiting for the blue hair dye to work its magic on my bleached roots. There's a shadow on the corner of my mouth. I turn my head slightly left, then slightly right. Weird. The shadow isn't moving. It slowly dawns on me that it's not a shadow that I'm looking at. It's a line caused by sagging skin. How did I miss this? When did this happen? What is happening to my face?

I had already had a few run-ins with my neck, which appeared to be growing rings like an aging tree. Not to mention the wobbly skin that I could never see in the mirror but somehow appeared on every selfie like a Magic Eye picture made flesh. But this . . . thing at the corner of my mouth? This was no wrinkle. This was no ring. This was gravity. Who beats gravity? No one! It's the hardest working force in showbiz!

I could accept the hot flashes, the shifting body fat patterns, the gray hairs. But for me, making peace with my aging face was—or I should say *is*—one of the most difficult parts of cronedom. Youth is sold to us like a commodity, used as a stand-in for beauty. Both are weaponized for use against the crone—who is old, which is a stand-in for *ugly*.

Not only do I discover new lines etched into my skin by the day, but they're now joined by the errant chin hair that only makes itself known when I catch it glistening in the sun while I'm out in public. With other people. And lacking tweezers. How did it sprout in the twenty minutes between when I last looked in the mirror and the drive to lunch? (Honestly, it is kinda magic.)

While we can conceal a lot of physical changes of approaching cronedom, our faces are just out there. Being seen. I see my face every day—brushing my teeth, putting on lipstick, staring into the abyss—and yet the changes in my reflection catch me completely off guard. One day I look like me, and the next day, I look like my mother. What gives? Is this some sort of mirror of Dorian Gray?

What I realized is that I don't normally *look* at my face. I look in the mirror, sure, but it's to brush my teeth or put on mascara or pluck one of those chin hairs. I don't really pay attention to what I look like. My brain just fills in the blank with who I've always been. So when I have time to look—*really look*, like when I'm sitting for five hours in the stylist's chair—I finally have the time and the space to face my (aging) face. And it's during this moment of shock that every terrible message that I've been spoon-fed about aging comes flooding in: WRINKLES = BAD! OLD = UGLY! LINES ARE FOR

COCAINE, NOT FACES! (Okay, that last one is courtesy of a very drunk friend in the bathroom at Gold-Diggers in East Hollywood circa 1998.) But if we can move past such messages, with the help of our crone touchstones, it's also possible to use these moments of sustained attention to feel a more intimate connection with what our faces look like in real life, right now.

You don't have to embrace your aging face. But getting to know it is a first step to coming to terms with it and accepting that it exists. Hold on to your mirrors, my friends, because things are going to get a little weird in here.

SPELL IT OUT

✴ I Scry with My Little Eye . . . ✴

Scrying is a divination technique that uses a reflective surface to help us gain insight and understanding. If you've ever seen a psychic staring into a crystal ball? That's scrying. It's a way to get in touch with our second sight. Scrying is typically used to look into the future. But we're going to use it more as an exercise in introspection and empowerment. We use peppermint in this spell because it's a healing herb that promotes wisdom and insight. The goal of this exercise is to become accustomed to your aging face, giving you new words to describe yourself.

YOU'LL NEED

* A wall-mounted mirror (like in your bathroom or a bedroom)
* Peppermint tea
* Sticky notes and a pen
* Your cell phone camera

THE RITUAL

1. Look at yourself in the mirror for ten to twenty seconds. Try not to make any judgments. Just study your reflection with your face at rest.
2. Take a sip of peppermint tea and return to your reflection. You can smile, or frown, or have a full resting witch face.
3. Using your sticky notes and pen, write two to three words that describe your face. You're not allowed to say anything judgmental or negative, and you're also not allowed to simply describe your physical features. So no *blue eyes* or *ugly* or *make an appointment for Botox*. Think words like *wise* or *open* or *guarded* or *pissed off* or *questioning*.
4. Affix the notes to the mirror, then snap a mirror selfie.
5. Put the notes in your grimoire, store them in an envelope (make sure to date them first), or toss them out if you don't care about keeping a record.

If you find yourself picking apart your reflection or find that there's no way for you to do this ritual without engaging in a lot of negative self-talk, it's best that you skip this one until you're ready!

AGING GRACELESSLY

People often praise women celebrities for *aging gracefully*—as in, they're visibly aging, but they somehow still look amazing. It's what every older woman is supposed to aspire to—and the only acceptable way for a woman to age, especially a woman in the public eye. So how does one age gracefully? If you ask the celebrities in question, they might say their secret is yoga, or olive oil, or bee pollen. But the real answer is "a hell of a lot of work."

When women are praised for aging gracefully, the unspoken implication is often that they're not getting a lot of cosmetic procedures—that they're embracing the natural aging process, but just happen to look incredible, naturally. And it's true that celebrities are likely to have some genetic gifts that keep them looking well-preserved! But what they really have is *better plastic surgeons* than the people whose work is obvious. Aging gracefully takes money (for Botox, fillers, plastic surgeons, personal trainers, nutritionists, aestheticians), it takes time (for research, consultations, appointments, recovery), it takes access to the right professionals (see: time and money), and it takes a hell of a lot of effort focused on a sole issue: trying to look younger than you are.

Graceful aging is like a prima ballerina dancing. She appears to effortlessly glide across the stage. But that grace comes at a high price: years of grueling practice, hobbled and bleeding feet, pain and injury.

So, crones, here's my suggestion: instead of aging gracefully, age gracelessly. There are just three commandments to remember. (Much easier than the other guy's ten.)

YOU DON'T HAVE TO DO ANYTHING TO YOUR FACE

Often when someone says "she's aging so gracefully," part of the subtext is "you could almost, though not quite, forget that she's aging at all." People like to be spared from thinking about the realities of age. But you don't need to get yourself injected with neurotoxins, or even smeared with retinoids, just to make the people around you more comfortable. Letting your face get old and weird can be extremely confrontational and punk in a society that would like to pretend aging women (especially visibly aging women) don't exist. If the graceful ager is a ballerina, you can be a bitch in combat boots. Get wrinkles! Get jowls! Make people deal with it!

BUT IF YOU WANT TO, GO FOR IT

Get Botox if you want! Get fillers! Get a facial made from the blood of six virgin Marines! (Maybe not that one.) It's your face, crone. Fuck it up however you want. Bless!

BUT IF YOU DO, DON'T LIE ABOUT IT

You don't have to tattoo BROUGHT TO YOU BY RESTYLANE on your forehead. (If it's smooth and immobile, we already know.) And you certainly don't owe anyone your medical history. However! One of the problems with the aging gracefully narrative is that *that's not what aging looks like.* By pretending their unlined faces and full lips are due to the miracle of nature and not Nurse Ellen with the needles, people who hide or gloss over their cosmetic procedures make it seem like everyone should be able to get them. Forehead lines become a personal failure instead of a normal part of the aging process. That's bad for everyone!

In a way, it's wild that I even have to say this. There's so much pressure to look young, so why should we feel like we're doing some kind of face crime if we get a touch of anti-wrinkle treatment? We're not supposed to age, but we're also not supposed to talk about what we do to prevent the signs of aging, but we're also not supposed to look like we've done anything to prevent the signs of aging? Can we *live*?

The thing is, a lot of people benefit from you feeling bad about your face. Anti-aging is a multi-multi-billion-dollar industry, supporting a whole network of injectors and surgeons and skin care companies. And, as I mentioned, you feel worse about your face when you're being led to believe that every other person except for you is somehow naturally looking smooth, taut, and well-rested. So, in the spirit of graceless aging, here's what the process looks like from the perspective of a crone who *is* letting science interfere with my looks and is *not* going to pretend otherwise!

First of all, I researched. A lot. (I also spent a lot of time looking in the mirror doing a version of the scrying spell!) I read reviews, I scrutinized before-and-after photos. I looked up doctors. I talked to friends. And then I made an appointment at a clinic specializing in dermal fillers.

I had a twenty-minute consultation, and then in the spirit of "my body, my science experiment," I went for it: I got fillers (in my cheeks, lips, and nasolabial folds, which affect the corner of the mouth) and Botox (in my forehead and laugh lines). Every seven to ten months, I return to get everything refreshed (which always means Botox and sometimes means fillers). It doesn't hurt that much—some places give you numbing cream—and it doesn't bruise too badly, but I'm not gonna lie, it does cost between hundreds and thousands of dollars every time. (You can sometimes chase discounts or get the face injections equivalent of a Blockbuster loyalty card, but this isn't really a place to pinch pennies.)

I never get told I'm aging gracefully, which seems to be reserved for celebrities (or people who say "fuck" much less than I do). But I often hear that I look good for my age. I usually respond that it just takes money. If people are curious, I tell them all the things I told you.

Maybe you think having work done cancels out my crone cred. (Maybe I sometimes think that too!) But I have to live in the same ageist society you do—and even worse, I work in television. (Ageism is alive and well everywhere, but it's *thriving* in Hollywood.) Looking just not-old enough that people are more inclined to hire me is worth it since it preserves my livelihood.

No matter how empowered a crone you are, no matter how kick-ass you feel, the reality is that people treat you better when they think you look younger. It's okay to hate that and also want that. It's even okay to devote money, effort, and time to it. If there's anything that unites all crones, it's the idea that *your body belongs to you*. But that doesn't mean you have to contribute to the myth that looking young is easy.

One way or another, you earned that face—so show your work. Let people see how time, experience, and gravity have affected you. Or let them know what it takes to fight back. Don't glide gracefully into aging! Charge in, or kick and scream—that's up to you. But whatever you do? Make it *loud*.

Kiss and Make Up

There are lots of makeup rules floating around for women over forty—avoid heavy foundation, don't wear shimmer, no black eyeliner. You've probably been reading this book for long enough to guess that you don't have to listen to any of them. (I have seven black eyeliners in my makeup bag right now! Granted, I almost never wear them anymore, but those are my emotional support black eyeliners.) Your skin may be changing, society's expectations of how you "should" look may be changing, but how you deal with that is truly up to you. Much like clothing, there is no "too old for this" when it comes to makeup. It is not your duty to look a certain way for anyone—and you certainly don't owe it to anyone to "look pretty," whatever that means.

But your crone era is a great chance to put your **Wisdom**, **Knowledge**, and **Fuck It** to work on your self-presentation, and that includes painting your face. If you've always wanted to try out liquid eyeliner, orange lipstick, aggressive contouring, or going without makeup altogether, there's never been a better time.

If you're nervous about trying out a new makeup look, remember: you have the crone power of invisibility! Take advantage of that superpower and try out all of the glitter eye shadow and green eyeliner and black lipstick your heart desires, confident in the knowledge that nobody is really looking (and if they are, you don't care what they think). If someone thinks you look bad or scary, put that to use. Cackle loudly until they back away. Add in some Latin-sounding curses while you're at it. They'll never bother you again.

CRONES SERVING FACE

Looking for some makeup inspo? Go back to your Style Mad Libs on page 51, or your crone colors on page 46. What colors, shapes (e.g., soft, chiseled, rounded), and finishes (e.g., matte, glossy, glittery) do those bring to mind? Or get inspired by some of these glam crone makeup looks!

GOTH GLAM

Inspiration: Morticia Addams (Anjelica Huston) in *The Addams Family*

* **Base:** Use a foundation a few shades lighter than your own, then contour dramatically. Set with a white or shimmery powder.
* **Eyebrows:** Black, strong, and arched
* **Eyes:** Black liquid or pencil liner, dark smoky shadow.
* **Lips:** Red, red, red
* **Look:** Haughty but amused

FUTURE GLAM

Inspiration: Aunty Entity (Tina Turner) in *Max Mad Beyond Thunderdome*

* **Base:** Light coverage foundation with shimmery highlights
* **Eyebrows:** Natural, but defined
* **Eyes:** A neutral smoky eye
* **Lips:** A natural pink shade, with a touch of gloss
* **Look:** Fierce

RETRO GLAM

Inspiration: Endora (Agnes Moorehead) in *Bewitched*

* **Base:** Light coverage foundation
* **Eyebrows:** Natural

* **Eyes:** Heavy blue shadow, black liquid liner for an exaggerated cat eye
* **Lips:** Red or coral
* **Look:** Up to something

> To transform your Endora look to Ursula from *The Little Mermaid*, swap out the natural brow for an extremely arched black brow.

Three Things a Crone Should Never Wear

Being a woman who ages wouldn't be so exhausting if society didn't continue to make it so exhausting. Honestly, *they're* the ones making it weird. But we've made it to the end of the chapter! We've discovered how our crone touchstones can be a guide when we're wrestling with the issues of aging in our crone era. We've conquered our closets, ruminated on our grays, and faced our faces. And while I've told you to do whatever you desire with your own personal sack of flesh, there is a final thought I'd like to leave you with. Here are the three things you should never wear:

1. **A SMILE BY REQUEST**
   Instead, try baring your fangs and cackling maniacally.

2. **THE MANTLE OF PATRIARCHY**
   It's the only thing that could ruin a caftan.

3. **SOMEONE ELSE'S EXPECTATIONS**
   Fuck it.

3

CRONE HOME

> "Girls want only one thing, and it's
> the *Practical Magic* house."
>
> —LANE MOORE, AUTHOR OF *HOW TO BE ALONE*

The older I get, the stronger my desire becomes to completely abandon my life for a witch's cottage deep in the woods. A place stuffed with dusty books and endless cups of tea, an overgrown herb garden, a clowder of cats, and a murder of crows. (It may take some magic to make them get along. I haven't totally figured that part out yet.). I wish I could be so bold. Or, more to the point, I wish I could afford to be so bold. Do you know the going rate on haunted cottages these days?

I'm clearly not the only crone who fantasizes about retreating to the woods. I think it's inspired by the crone voice we all have, the one that whispers (or screams) *you don't have to do this, you could just leave.* It's our collective crone touchstone of **Fuck It**, reverberating through our bodies like a witchy spidey-sense. We're itching to break up with society before it breaks up with us first.

But what is it about this specific fantasy? Though the details may differ—maybe the cats are dogs, maybe the cottage is on a cliff by the sea—so many crones seem to harbor a vision of their ideal future that's almost exactly like mine. The cottage speaks to our need for a room of our own. The desire to be surrounded by quiet nature reflects our growing appreciation of solitude and our waning interest in what other people think. Paging through dusty books and sipping tea while a murder of crows does our bidding? Books and crows (or any animal friends) are excellent companions who rarely play devil's advocate. And tea—well, a crone has got to stay hydrated. Together it adds up to a place where no one requires or expects anything of us. A place where we can *simply exist.* A crone paradise.

But, alas, we live in the actual world. And the thing about the actual world? It's incredibly difficult to escape. It requires money. Even if you have money, movers will want an address beyond "Crone's Cottage, Woods." And thanks to climate change, a lot of the woods are on fire right now. (It doesn't matter when you're reading this. The woods are on fire.) So for most of us, disappearing into the woods isn't a practical solution.

Which is good, because now I can admit that I'm not the hugest fan of tea. And dust is hell on my allergies. Do the woods even have Wi-Fi? And I need indoor plumbing, because these old bones are *not* trudging through the snow at 3:48 a.m. when my bladder comes knocking.

So while our cottage in the woods may be better in theory than practice, there are other ways for us to conjure our ultimate crone lifestyle!

IN THIS CHAPTER, WE'LL LEARN:

* How to create the witch cottage of your dreams—even if you rent!
* What to plant in your crone garden—even if you have a black thumb
* The best uses for herbs, in and out of the kitchen
* How to conjure a cocktail
* How to determine your perfect familiar

The Crone's Nest

Think back to the first place you felt was truly yours as an adult. Maybe it was your dorm room at college. Or the duplex you shared with friends. Or the room you rented in an apartment with a stranger you found on Craigslist. (How is that a thing we used to do?) Do you remember how it felt the first time you walked in?

After graduating from film school, I moved to Los Angeles. My first apartment was in a three-story stucco building painted a muted yellow. The elevator was always broken, the fake plants in the atrium were covered in dust, and every Saturday morning my neighbor would shoo her kids into the open-air corridor, telling them to "run it out."

But none of that mattered. It was my own place. (That I shared with a roommate. Who I met at the animal shelter, not on Craigslist!) I remember what I saw walking through the door for the very first time. The blank walls that called out for artwork. The (faux) granite countertops, waiting for cute kitchen knickknacks. And that empty threshold, ready for a welcome mat that spoke to my personality but wasn't trying too hard.

I had plans for that place. I was going to take that anonymous off-white box and transform it into my personal sanctuary! Which meant I couldn't just fill it with "stuff." Every piece would be selected with intention. Whether it was a kitchen table, pillowcase, or bread knife, it would contribute to my overarching vision.

But I was working as an agent's assistant at ICM. I earned $400 a week, before taxes, without overtime. (Oh, I worked overtime. But I didn't get paid overtime. It was considered "voluntary." Hollywood in the '90s!) After paying rent, utilities, and my car note, there wasn't much money left over. My sixty- to eighty-hour work weeks weren't leaving me much in the time or energy department, either.

Sure, I still selected things with intention. It's just that my intention became "whatever's cheap and clean so I'm not sleeping on the floor." I bought a mattress from a guy who sold them out of his pickup truck, which was parked at an abandoned gas station. My sofa was a tan and forest-green monstrosity, a floor model from a furniture store that was going out of business. (The free throw pillows were covered in a print called Aztec Fire.) My kitchen table hailed from IKEA and was flanked by three black plastic folding chairs. And my mismatched cutlery? I discovered it at a yard sale while walking my dog. (RIP, Thurber.)

FOR NOW TO FOREVER

I kept telling myself that these purchases were just "for now." That one day I'd make more money, and then I could decorate the home of my dreams. Or maybe I'd have more time to hunt for deals, hit up the resale stores, even maybe craft some pieces of my own. But "for now" has a way of turning into "for the unforeseeable future."

It's been nearly three decades since that first apartment. I eventually made more money. At one point, I even managed to buy a home. I no longer have to buy mattresses at abandoned gas stations. I'm better about designing a living space that I love and that reflects who I am. But there are still times that I get something "for now" because I need something now.

If you have some "for nows" in your home—a duvet cover you don't love but that was on sale, a dining room set you inherited from your in-laws that isn't totally your style but was free—you don't have to worry that they'll stand in the way of manifesting your ideal crone home. There's nothing wrong with good-enough furnishings! We all need stuff. But putting some thought and intent into how you decorate and arrange your home—without replacing anything, or even necessarily buying anything—can help those "for nows" feel more like "for yous."

There's a wealth of ways for every one of us to bring more magic into our home. We'll begin with simple, temporary changes and get more advanced as we head through the chapter. So whether you rent or own, whether you're on a budget or the sky's the limit, whether you want to tackle one room or the entire lair, it's time to manifest the crone's cottage of your dreams!

Cottage in a Carryall

Cottage in a Carryall is the "Bed in a Bag" for crones. In case you never made it into a Bed Bath & Beyond, Bed in a Bag is all the linens required to outfit a bed (fitted sheet, top sheet, two pillow cases) in one bag. Similarly, Cottage in a Carryall is a portable collection of items that conjure crone vibes. No tools required, and it doesn't permanently mark your space. (Unless one of your items is haunted. Your mileage may vary.) You can even bring it with you on vacation, to make a generic hotel room (or your mother-in-law's house, or whatever) feel more like home. It's great for personalizing desks, bedside tables, and countertops. The starter pack includes:

* Scarf (for draping)
* Heavy mug (for teas and libations)
* Small box, preferably ornate (for crystals, charms, or meds)
* Cedarwood or sandalwood incense or potpourri (for a woodsy smell)
* Collection of dead sticks in a vase (for cool shadows and crone vibes)
* Enchanted animal figurine, representing your familiar (for talking to)
* Sound effects app, with crackling fireplace or howling wind
* Black or purple cell phone cozy (for hiding your phone)
* Bag to keep everything in—try a Mary Poppins–style tapestry bag (pre-Disney Mary Poppins was definitely a crone), a tote from your favorite weird museum, or just a large shopping bag

For crones who have a bit more space, try the Cottage in a Corner expansion pack! This contains everything from the Cottage in a Carryall, plus the following.

* One of three chair styles:
    · Comfy chair, for the classic tea-drinking, book-reading crone
    · Rocking chair, preferably creaky, for the contemplative crone
    · Throne chair, for the commanding crone who loves a seated power pose
* Thick blanket, preferably knitted by yourself or a local gnome
* Cauldron (for meds that don't fit in your small ornate box)
* Broomstick (for flying or swatting your roomie out of your space)

Divine Drapes

One of the basics found in every crone's bag of tricks is the silk scarf. The scarf is the multi-tool of witchcraft—it can transform any space. Drape it over a desk to use as an instant altar. Drape it over your head as a veil for divination rituals. Drape it over a table to use as a foundation for tarot card readings. Are you sensing a pattern here? Crones love draping, and nothing's drapier than . . . drapes. Curtains are an easy way to drama to any crone abode.

Begin by figuring out your fabric style.

* **Crones who thrive in the light:** Pick a light, flowy drape. Look for sheer or viscose. Think Princess Diana's twenty-five-foot wedding dress train, but haunted.
* **Crones who thrive in the dark:** Select a dark, heavy drape. Velvet and damask are ideal. Think of the night of the new moon, inky black and still.

* **Crones who can't choose:** Go with a double drape, with the lighter curtain material closer to the window and the heavier one closer to the room's interior. You contain multitudes!

Of course, you can purchase ready-made curtains (cheaper) or have custom drapes made (pricier). But if you're looking to conjure a curtain with a little more personal magic? Read on!

CURTAINS FOR YOU!

Want a custom curtain without the cursed price? Create your own! Don't worry if you're not blessed with crafty magic—drapes are one of the easiest DIY projects in existence.

Home economics was a requirement at my junior high—a requirement that I almost failed because I could not sew. I wasn't only terrified of tanking my GPA; we were also supposed to wear our creations in the seventh-grade fashion show. I had nightmares about my skirt falling off mid-walk, effectively pantsing myself. So I smuggled my skirt home and had my mom finish it. I told her not to make it "too good." She told me not to worry. My skirt stayed on, my GPA took a small hit, and I never sat in front of a sewing machine again.

Enter the magic of Stitch Witchery. Stitch Witchery is a weblike material that can bond two pieces of fabric when heat (an iron) is applied. It's cheap and it can be found at most big box stores. (You can use anything called "iron-on interfacing," "fusible interfacing," or "iron-on hem tape"—I just like the brand name Stitch Witchery for obvious reasons.) This works best on lighter fabrics, and when using a thin curtain rod.

1. To figure out how much fabric you'll need, measure from the curtain rod to just above the floor. (Usually curtains usually fall about half an inch above the floor, but you do you.) Make sure you add a few extra inches to your curtain length for your hem and to create the loop where your

curtains thread through the curtain rod. (Have the fabric store cut each curtain piece rather than buying one big bolt and cutting it yourself!)

2. Arrange your fabric somewhere where it's safe to use an iron.

3. For the hem, place a strip of your Stitch Witchery (or other interfacing) an inch or two from the bottom of the fabric. Fold the fabric up so it covers the strip, then iron.

4. Fold a piece of fabric from the top to create a tunnel. It's basically like creating a hem, but you want to make sure there's space for the curtain rod to slide through. Add your strip of Stitch Witchery to connect the bottom of the tunnel (make sure not to fuse the whole thing closed), iron, and voilà! Curtains!

If nothing at the fabric store speaks to you, get thee to the thrift store (or resale shop). If you're less than crafty, look for items that are easy to mod: top sheets, pillow shams, tablecloths, flags. But if you've got a bit more know-how, or you're willing to learn? The thrift store is a virtual treasure chest. For the crafty crone who wants a little more haunt in her house, I recommend creating a *cursed curtain*.

Cursed curtains are made of fabrics with a terrible story to tell.

* **Wedding dresses:** No item of clothing contains more hopes and dreams than a wedding dress. And now that dress is hanging limply from a hanger at your local Goodwill. A runaway bride? Jilted at the altar? Messy divorce? Has she moved onto the next astral plane? Make wedding dress drapes and turn your house into Miss Havisham's haven!

  Bonus: Plenty of material

  Haunting grade: B+

* **Graduation gowns:** Another symbol of hopes and dreams, but also of nightmares like crushing student loan debt and lukewarm job markets.

Normally made of shiny synthetic fabrics that don't breathe well. Curtains may appear less crone and more community theater.

Bonus: You can easily stage *Macbeth* in your house

Haunting grade: C

* **Single faded sheet with clown print and rust-colored stain:** Run.

Bonus: I TOLD YOU TO RUN!

Haunting grade: A++++

If none of these suit, you can choose any fabric that speaks to you, even if it's not *literally* speaking to you due to demonic possession.

With our drapery sorted, let's move on to something slightly less terrifying, though only slightly: the blank wall.

Un-Blank Your Walls

Any writer will tell you there are few things scarier than the blank page. Sometimes I'll just type nonsense so I don't have to watch the cursor blinking against a screen of white space, watching. Listening. Judging.

I feel the same way when I'm confronted with a blank wall. Yes, you can do anything with a blank wall. But if anything is possible, that means you have to consider everything. I could paint. But what color? What finish? What is semigloss? I could hang artwork. But should it be framed? Unframed? Do I have a hook strong enough to hold it? How the hell do you use a stud finder? How do you make a gallery wall? What about murals? Supergraphics? Could I cover the whole place in tin foil? (You can, but it's pricey and people will assume you believe the moon landing was faked.)

The state I spin myself into when faced with too many options is what I call the Grim Bog of Indecision. I can do anything, so I do nothing. As each day passes, the pressure to do the exact perfect thing with the walls increases because I've waited too long. My panic turns to dread as I sink deeper into the Grim Bog.

The blank white walls—now somehow blanker and whiter—are always watching. Listening. Judging.

If you're someone who succumbs to the Grim Bog of Indecision, it turns out there is a cure. It's actually the same technique I use to deal with the blank page: typing some nonsense, just so there's something there. You can use this as a decorating tactic, too.

Just put something on the wall. Anything. Hang your poster of Robert Smith, tape up a to-go menu, a religious tract, a flier from the union rally. Use washable colored pencils and draw a mural, a pentagram, a self-portrait. Pull yourself out of the bog, throw some nonsense on the wall, and let's get to crone-ifying our casa.

THE EASY ENCHANTMENT OF AN ACCENT WALL

The accent wall is perfect for crones who don't have the time or budget to cover every inch of wall space. If you're able to paint in your place, choose one wall that you want to feature—it might be an architecturally interesting one (maybe it has a fireplace, if so I'm jealous), or it's a wall you can see through the doorways of other rooms, or maybe it's just the one that the light hits perfectly in the afternoon. Highlight that wall with a bold color, while leaving the other walls neutral. This is also perfect if you want to live with a wall color before you fully commit to painting the whole place. But paint isn't the only option for your accent wall!

Wallpaper was the first DIY project I attempted as a single crone. Everyone insisted I'd need a second pair of hands, but if you're patient and you have an exacting eye (to line up patterns from sheet to sheet) you'll fly right through.

- Peel-and-stick wallpaper doesn't damage the walls, which is ideal for crones who rent.
- No matter your category of crone style, a wallpaper exists for you. Spooky midcentury modern? Witchy maximalist? Cryptid Cape Cod? Goth Hollywood regency? (Me.) It's all out there.
- If you can dream it, you can buy it. If you can't find exactly what you want, there are websites that will let you design your own prints.
- Order samples before purchasing a full roll of wallpaper.
- Beware: once you start, you'll want to cover your whole house!

Fabric can also be used to create an accent wall. But it can be pricier than its paper counterpart.

- If you don't care about damaging your walls, use a staple gun or hot-glue gun to affix the fabric to the wall.
- If you rent, use double-sided tape, tacks, or small nails to hold the fabric in place.
- Fabric stretches more easily than wallpaper, so pay attention as you work so you don't end up with loose pockets of fabric (unless you want that!)
- Beware: the type of fabric you use can affect the room's temperature! When I was an assistant, I once helped my boss cover her office walls in red velvet. It looked like a bordello for djinn. It felt like a tropical rainforest.

YOUR ARCANE ART GALLERY

I may have invented haunted drapery, but haunted paintings have existed for ages. You might have seen Bill Stoneham's 1972 painting *The Hands Resist Him*, which went viral in 2000 when it was posted on eBay alongside claims that it was cursed. The painting depicts the artist as a young boy, standing next to a doll in front of a glass-paneled door. Small hands can be seen pressing against the glass door behind him—which is creepy enough on its own, but the eBay seller also insisted that the characters would fight, move, or leave the frame at night. But this was not by any means the first haunted painting, though it might be the most internet-famous! For instance, the central figure of the 1899 Edvard Munch painting *Death and the Child* is also said to disappear from her frame, and visitors to the museum where it hangs report that her eyes follow you around the room. (This is just a well-known perceptual effect, but never mind.)

Establish your own arcane gallery by adorning your walls with haunted paintings, pictures, and photos. While it may take a bit of searching to find a cursed canvas, you'll know it when you see it.

Signs an artwork is haunted:

* Each time you visit, it hangs in a different place.
* Customers avoid it at all costs, calling it "creepy."
* The face of the clerk who stocked it has gone blurry, and instead of saying "have a nice day," he lets out a guttural wail.
* They offer you money to take it.
* It's propped up against a dumpster with a sign that reads HAUNTED!

Don't have access to haunted artwork? Create your own!

DIY COUNTERFEIT CURSED CANVAS

In the mid-2010s there was a whole trend of gluing googly eyes on things. Upon seeing them stuck to a planter at brunch, I wondered aloud: What if googly eyes were from a real living creature, but people didn't know? It was the last time my friend brought her daughter to brunch.

In the spirit of this fad, and in remembrance of all the googly-eyed creatures who gave up their sight for it, you're going to take an existing painting (or picture, or print) and add your own cursed imagery. Paint, pencil, sketch, or decoupage—this is time for the crafty crone to shine!

* Add a hellmouth to Monet's haystacks!
* Insert a subtle extra arm into Klimt's *The Kiss*!
* Your favorite cryptid lurking in the background turns *American Gothic* into American Goth!
* There's a whole aftermarket of modified Thomas Kinkade paintings—to which people have added aliens, succubi, Cthulhu, and other fun supernatural beings—to gain inspiration from.

Your art won't actually be haunted, but it'll appear that way. And who knows? It might eventually become possessed. A crone can dream!

Mini Home Makeover

If thinking about creating the crone home of your dreams still leaves you feeling more overwhelmed than exhilarated, or you feel the Grim Bog of Indecision about to swallow you whole? Break it down by location. Dressing up one key spot may make the rest of your project feel approachable—or you may decide that one spot is all you need.

FRONT DOOR

As the saying goes, you only get one chance to make a first impression. Here's a few suggestions to make sure the impression of you is accurate.

* A wreath made of sticks, or dried herbs like mint, lavender, and rosemary, creates an inviting entrance. You can make these yourself using floral wire and a wreath form from a craft or garden store.
* If you're not feeling up for company, a wreath made of animal bones and crow feathers works wonders. (Plastic bones will be easier to source.)
* Keep a decorative box of salt at the front door for an extra layer of protec-

tion (and for salting your front steps in winter).

* Invest in a doormat that speaks to you—whether that's one that says WEL-COME or exactly the opposite. Halloween is a great time to find doormats featuring bats, snakes, or eyeballs, and since they're "seasonal" items (for *some* people) they often go on sale in November.

KITCHEN

Whether you work magic in the kitchen or you're the queen of takeout, every crone can use these kitchen basics!

* Cauldrons may be less practical than stock pots for your potions and stews, but you can use a decorative cauldron to store cooking implements —or chopsticks for your takeout sushi.
* Ornate wall and ceiling hooks are the ideal addition to a crone kitchen. Use them for dish towels, to dry fresh herbs, or to hang your witch's hat.
* Store cool-looking bottles (empty or full), your favorite glassware, and jars of dry goods on open shelves or countertops for an apothecary feel.
* The point about Halloween doormats goes double for kitchenware! High-end home goods stores often stock cool plates, cutlery, and serving items featuring crone-appropriate imagery (crows, skeletons, etc.) in October. Snag them on sale and they'll work year-round.

BEDROOM

Whether the bedroom is your personal sanctuary or the place where the real magic happens (or both), add instant hex appeal with these simple decor ideas.

* A collection of pretty jars on your dresser is a charming way to store your amulets, crystals, potions, and notions.
* Swap your utilitarian bedside water bottle for a ceremonial chalice—or just a cuter water bottle.

* Drape translucent scarves over your lampshades (make sure they're not touching the bulb) for a cozier glow—and darker shadows.
* Sure, that blanket's nice, but you know what would be even better? Two blankets! If you can crochet, knit, or quilt, you can load up your living space with bedspreads and throws. (If you can't, you might want to learn!)
* Treat yourself to an ornate mirror for glamour spells—just don't listen if it tells you you're not the fairest in the land.

Kitschy Witch

Put the finishing touches on your crone abode with mystical trinkets, arcane objects, and curiosities. Keep an eye out for keepsakes that suit your particular crone style.

* **If you're a creepy crone:** Broken dolls, taxidermy, animal bones, wet specimens, skeleton keys, funeral urns, antique medical implements
* **If you're a mystical crone:** Candles, tapestries, broomsticks, tarot cards, Ouija boards, crystals and crystal balls
* **If you're a bog witch:** Terrariums, insects in shadow boxes, real or fake plants, preserved moss, anything mushroom-shaped
* **If you're a cozy crone:** Old books, antique tea sets, handmade lace runners, pocket watches, pillows and throws

It's okay if your witch's cottage (or room, or corner of your shared living space) isn't for everybody. Because it's not supposed to be for everybody. It's for you.

Baba Yaga

It would be a crime to write a book about crones and not write about our patron saint: Baba Yaga. The ancient witch of Slavic lore resides deep in the woods. Her hut is perched atop chicken legs and surrounded by a fence crowned with human skulls. Instead of a broomstick, Baba Yaga flies around in a giant mortar, using the pestle to steer, like a magical stick shift.

Say what you want, the witch has got style.

Being a crone who's opted for an alternative woods lifestyle, Baba Yaga attracts her share of criticism. Most of it boils down to: she's ugly. Because ugly is the worst thing you can call a woman. But do you think Baba Yaga gives a single chicken-legged fuck what anyone thinks? Of course not! She's tapped out. She's living in her weird little hut, coexisting with wildlife and flying around in her stick-shift mortar and pestle. This witch is living the dream.

What happens when the wayward traveler shows up at her door? Sometimes Baba Yaga helps them on their way. But usually, she fries up their flesh and uses their femurs as fence posts. I mean, come on. What did they think was going to happen? The woman lives in a hut on chicken legs surrounded by a fence of bones. Why would you *bother* her? Forget FAFO. When it comes to Baba Yaga, it's all about FAFU: Fuck Around, (get) Fried Up.

Garden Crone

A key element to conjuring the crone cottage of your dreams is incorporating elements from nature. If we can't live out the rest of our crone days in the woods, then we bring the woods to us. I know this can cause anxiety for a lot of us. I used to apologize in advance to the plants in my car on the way home from the nursery. But with time and a learning curve that wasn't as steep as I'd have liked, I learned to tend to my plant friends. So don't worry if you're a crone with a thumb as black as your heart. There's a plant for that!

Since not every crone has access to outdoor space, I'm focusing on plants that can be grown in containers indoors. But you can also grow these plants outside if you have a yard, balcony, green roof, or community garden—or when you get that cottage in the woods.

A CRONE'S GUIDE TO GOTHIC HOUSEPLANTS

Listen, this witch loves a basic potted plant. I dragged a ficus and a fern from apartment to apartment until I abandoned them to a roommate who could raise them both much better than I. I once killed a boyfriend's cactus because I loved (watered) it too much. But sometimes, I want to grow something a little less basic and a little more me: dark, odd-looking, poisonous if consumed.

If plants go into hiding when you walk into a garden center, or you're wanted in seventeen states for being a serial plant killer? Artificial plants are the way to go. They've come a long way since the first fake plastic tree. I won't judge. But if you're interested in raising some spooky plant children, read on.

> Many of the plants in this section are poisonous. So if you have pets, small children, or specters who cannot keep their ghost mitts to themselves, take the necessary precautions to keep them safe.

GOTH HOUSEPLANT STARTER PACK

Featuring burgundy, purple, or dark green leaves, these plants are perfect for the crone who's just getting her gnarled feet wet when it comes to plant care.

Burgundy rubber plant (*Ficus elastica* 'Burgundy'): **Featuring dark green leaves with a burgundy tint, this rubber plant can grow up to eight feet tall!**

* Thrives in full sunlight and well-draining soil
* Make sure that the soil dries completely between waterings.
* Keep the leaves dust-free by wiping them with a damp cloth. (Dust can actually interfere with the growing process.)

Ripple peperomia (*Peperomia caperata*): **With its burgundy, heart-shaped leaves and spiky flower stems, the ripple peperomia looks like it should be headlining a goth metal festival.**

* Does best in medium to bright indirect light (like a vampire, it burns in direct sunlight)
* Like the rubber plant, enjoys well-draining soil
* Don't let it dry out! The soil should be kept moist.

Purple velvet plant (*Gynura aurantiaca*): **Featuring fuzzy purple leaves with jagged edges, this plant probably shopped at Hot Topic. (No shade!)**

* Prefers bright, indirect sunlight (like I said, no shade!)
* Plant in well-draining soil.
* Water when the top inch or so of soil is dry.

Hoya rosita (*Hoya wayetii x tsangii*): **Its dark green and maroon leaves turn red when it's stressed out (specifically, when it's sun stressed, or getting too**

much sunlight). Perfect for the communication fiends who like to know when people (or plants) are angry at them.

* Tougher to find, but unlike most rare plants, it's easy to care for
* Enjoys bright indirect light (the stress from direct light is what causes its leaves to change color!)
* Requires well-draining soil
* Water when the soil has completely dried out.

GOTH HOUSEPLANTS, CARNIVORE EDITION

Looking to level up? These carnivorous plants are fussier to care for but add a delightfully creepy touch to your indoor potted plant menagerie. While they do well in pots, carnivorous plants thrive in humid conditions, making them perfect for a terrifying terrarium. Once again, most of these are poisonous, so use care.

Venus flytrap (*Dionaea muscipula*): With its signature gaping jaws that clamp down on unsuspecting insects, the Venus flytrap is probably the most recognizable of the carnivorous plants in the United States.

* Its light needs fluctuate depending on the season. From spring to fall, it requires twelve hours of sunlight a day, with at least four hours of full sun.
* Water with distilled water (or rainwater) from the bottom by placing the plant's pot in a tray of water.
* Over winter, the Venus flytrap goes through a dormant phase where it requires no light and no food. Move it to a colder location (between 40 and 50 degrees Fahrenheit—not freezing!) and water only when the tray goes completely dry.
* Feed it live insects by dropping them into the plant's "jaws." Gently stimulate flytrap's trigger hairs (aka "teeth") to aid in digestion. Aww!

Cobra lily (*Darlingtonia californica*): Named for the fact that it looks like a group of rearing cobras. Adorable!

* Prefers "bog-like conditions" (me too), so keep it moist!
* Skip the tap water—rainwater or distilled water only.
* Bright indirect sunlight during the spring and summer months, and decreasing light in winter
* Plant in peat moss or perlite.
* Feed it insects on occasion by dropping them directly in the plant's mouth.

Butterwort (*Pinguicula*): If a succulent and flypaper had a baby, it would be the butterwort.

* Enjoys direct sunlight (but not too much—it can burn!)
* Well-draining soil and watering from below is recommended.
* While it's the least finicky of our carnivorous trio, it's still a water snob: rainwater or distilled water only.
* Since butterworts catch insects on the surface of their sticky leaves, it's easy to see if they're eating.
* If it's not catching anything, you can feed it. But no more than one insect a week! Even if it's been good.

HANGING GARDEN WALL

Looking for something more complex than an indoor container garden? Consider a plant wall or vertical garden. A lush plant wall can feel like having a whole garden indoors, a space where your life as a crone in nature and life as a crone in your cottage collide. Vining or climbing plants are best for plant walls, but if you want to bring in branches and sticks to literally live in the woods, no one's stopping you!

* You can find ready-made vertical garden kits at gardening and home improvement stores.
* Determined to DIY? Hanging shoe organizers work great as a base. (This also is a great solution for renters!)
* Black thumb? Renter? Fake it with artificial plants. No watering means no mess! Mount a piece of lattice-top fencing to your wall, then weave your artificial plant, branches, or vines through the lattice. Feeling extra? Spray-paint your greenery purple. Or silver. Or black, like my heart.

HOUSEHOLD HERBS FOR THE EVERYDAY WITCH

Herbs are the foundation of every crone garden—and their uses go well beyond cooking. They can be steeped in teas, infused in essential oils, and burned in sacred spells. (But I mostly just use them for cooking.) If you don't want to grow your own, then as honorary crone Ina Garten says: *store-bought is fine.* But note that some of these applications are more appropriate for fresh herbs and some are better for dried—and if you're cooking, remember that the flavor of dried herbs is about three times more intense than fresh, so you'll need less.

> None of these suggestions constitute medical advice!
> I'm a crone, not a doctor!

ROSEMARY

The Swiss army knife of witchy herbs. It's used in cleansing magic, protection rituals, and love spells. Or: she protec, but she also attrac.

* **Make it magic:** Feeling weighed down by negative energy? A few sprigs of fresh rosemary added to your bath is a simple purification ritual.

* **Make it makeup:** Rub rosemary oil into your scalp to take your crone mane from stringy to strong.
* **Make it a meal:** Rosemary and chicken are made for each other. But if you're looking for a meatless option, adding rosemary to your bread dough will make you the most popular crone on the block.

BASIL

In the third century BCE, Greek philosopher Chrysippus wrote that basil "exists only to drive men insane." So yeah, it's pretty much the MVP of crone herbs. Basil is used in attraction spells (think money and love). Plus it's the foundation of a classic pesto.

* **Make it magic:** Tuck a sachet of basil in your pocket before asking for a raise, or keep a basil plant by the cash register of your store.
* **Make it makeup:** Basil extract is supposed to be super moisturizing and reduce the appearance of wrinkles. You can buy basil oil or make your own by infusing coconut oil with dried basil.
* **Make it a meal:** Pesto is magic because you can't really mess it up. You take your ingredients (fresh basil, garlic, pine nuts, parmesan cheese, and olive oil), pop 'em in a food processor, give 'em a whiz, and blammo! Pesto! Sometimes I skip the pine nuts (pricey) or add baby spinach for a thicker pesto to use as a dip or for stuffing baked mushroom caps.

BAY LEAF

The bay leaf is the Psychic Friends Network of herbs: it's believed to boost psychic powers, opening up our third eye—the "sight beyond sight." While the bay leaf comes from a tree, bay laurel grows well in a pot indoors, so you can always have leaves at the ready. Tucking a bay leaf under your pillow is said to promote dream divination. What can't bay leaf do?

* **Make it magic:** About to embark on an intense conversation? Slip a fresh bay leaf in your pocket or bra to home in on your intuition and second sight.
* **Make it makeup:** Bay leaf is said to have anti-inflammatory properties, useful as a topical treatment for treating sunburn and psoriasis.
* **Make it a meal:** Dried bay leaf is the secret ingredient in soup, stews, and braises. The leaf itself isn't consumed—it's added at the beginning of cooking, then removed before eating. Bay leaf adds a complex, slightly bitter flavor to whatever it's added to.

Eye of Newt, Toe of Frog, and a Hint of Cinnamon

Crones of legend have been known to indulge in a bit of cannibalism—and sometimes more than a bit. Slavic crone Baba Yaga feasts on stolen children and travelers who dare disturb her in her chicken-legged cottage. Hansel and Gretel's grizzled old crone in the German fairy tale attempted to turn them into Sunday roast. In Japanese folklore, the yamauba are mountain hags who present as welcoming old ladies by day, then appear in their true hideous form to eat their guests by night. But cannibalism isn't just cliché, it's impractical. (And what about vegan crones?)

Don't worry—not every crone of yore was a one-stop human butcher shop! You might be familiar with the 1975 children's book Strega Nona, written and illustrated by Tomie dePaola (but based on a much older folk tale). Strega Nona (Italian for "Grandma Witch") is the town crone who provides medicines, plays matchmaker, and cooks mounds of spaghetti in her magical pasta pot. Apologies to my own baba (RIP), but I'm heading to Strega Nona's for dinner.

Kitchen witchery is my favorite kind of magic. There's nothing I love more than making food for friends. The first time I cooked Christmas dinner, it was for fifteen people. I can conjure a cocktail party out of my pantry with six types of hors d'oeuvres and a signature drink in an hour.

But I didn't grow up knowing how to cook. My mom kept me out of the kitchen—intentionally. She was born in a displaced persons camp just after the second world war. There were no real options for her outside of getting married and having children. So her plan for me was not to teach me any of the homemaking arts. No cooking. No baking. No cleaning. No laundry. No sewing, no mending, no knitting, no crocheting.

I managed to get through college without having to even boil an egg, but when I moved out to Los Angeles, I was lost. So I did what any good nerd does: I researched. I studied cooking techniques. I practiced recipes. I started with things that were cheap and probably wouldn't kill me if I didn't prepare them correctly: pastas and veggie soups. I graduated to fish and red meat, and, finally, chicken. (Handling raw chicken still squicks me out. I'm cringing as I write this.)

I still can't sew on a button or hem a pair of pants. I can't knit a hat or crochet a . . . whatever it is you crochet. A doily? But I can cook. And what's more magical than food? Recipes are real-life potions and spells. Cookbooks, a grimoire of edible delights. I never feel closer to my cauldron-stirring sisters than when I'm standing over a vat of chicken soup, wooden spoon in hand.

Strega Nona

Strega Nona, star of Tomie dePaola's classic 1975 children's book of the same name, is the flip side of Baba Yaga. Strega Nona is the kind, wise crone, the village grandma who doles out medicine, advice, and heaping bowls of spaghetti from her magic pot. The magic pot is the main tool of Strega Nona's magic. When she sings to it, it overflows with spaghetti. To stop the pasta production, she blows three kisses at it.

In dePaola's book, the old witch hires a young man named Big Anthony to help her around the house. She tells him there's only one rule: no touching the magic pot. But one night Big Anthony sees Strega Nona making pasta and thinks *I could do that*.

He gets his chance with the magic pot when Strega Nona goes out of town. However, Big Anthony only knows how to make the spaghetti, He doesn't know how to stop it. Strega Nona returns home to discover the village covered in spaghetti. After blowing three kisses to the pot to stop the pasta production, she turns to the angry townsfolk. They want to get rid of Big Anthony for his misdeeds, but Strega Nona intervenes. She suggests Big Anthony clean up the village—by eating all the spaghetti.

Strega Nona's judgment is considered wise because the punishment fits the crime. But I think it's much more than that. Getting rid of Big Anthony makes the problem go away. But by making him stick around? He's a daily reminder to never underestimate a crone's powers —and always heed their warnings.

If cooking is magic, then chicken noodle soup should be the first listing in our recipe grimoire. Chicken noodle soup isn't just about the meal, it's about what it represents: Soothing care. Kindness. Healing. And it really does heal you, whether that's because of actual medicinal properties (as recent studies have suggested) or just the placebo effect, which is a kind of magic in itself. Plus it perfectly encapsulates the crone culinary arts:

* It's cooked in a cauldron (okay, a big pot).
* It's an easy way to feed your entire crone coven—
* —but if you're crone solo, it freezes and reheats beautifully.
* It has curative properties.
* It contains magical herbs.
* And it's practically folkloric!

If you don't have your own chicken noodle soup recipe, I offer you mine.

A CRONE'S CHICKEN NOODLE SOUP

This can be made vegetarian by skipping the chicken and using no-chicken broth, but I'd recommend the next recipe instead.

* A couple of glugs of olive oil
* 8 cloves of garlic, minced
* 1 large or 2 small sweet onions, diced
* 5–6 large carrots, cut into thick disks
* 3–4 celery stalks, chopped
* 2–3 tablespoons fresh ginger, peeled and chopped (use a tablespoon of ground ginger if that's all you've got)
* A few shakes of ground turmeric, to taste
* 1½–2 pounds bone-in chicken breast or thighs (I remove the skin first)

- * 4–8 cups of low-sodium chicken broth (depending on how brothy you like it)
- * 1 bay leaf
- * 3 sprigs of fresh rosemary
- * 3 sprigs of fresh thyme
- * Salt and pepper, to taste
- * 2 boxes (32 ounces) of your favorite dried pasta (I use fusilli)
- * 1 lemon

1. Heat your oil, then add garlic, onions, carrots, and celery, and sauté for about 5 to 7 minutes. (The onions will start to look translucent.)
2. Add ginger and turmeric, and sauté for about 30 seconds. (You want to make sure they get all up in your veggies.)
3. Add chicken, broth, bay leaf, rosemary, thyme, and salt and pepper to the pot. Make sure the chicken pieces are fully covered by the liquid. (It's okay if they peek out a teeny bit.)
4. Bring liquid to a boil, then turn the heat down, cover, and let simmer for 45 minutes, or until chicken is cooked through.
5. Remove chicken pieces from your pot with a slotted spoon and shred the meat with a fork (it should easily fall off the bone—be careful, it's hot!). Add meat back to the pot. Save bones for rituals or discard.
6. Add pasta to the pot and cook according to package directions (probably 8 to 10 minutes).
7. When noodles are cooked, squeeze fresh lemon over the pot.
8. Salt and pepper to taste.
9. Ladle soup into a bowl made of the skull of your enemy *or* a regular bowl and enjoy!

CRONE-Y MINESTRONE

Minestrone is a vegetarian (and easily vegan) dish that has all the magical vibes of chicken noodle soup, but without the meat. Think of this recipe as a jumping-off point. You can also add kale, zucchini, spinach, or whatever other vegetables need to make a quick exit from your refrigerator.

* A couple of glugs of olive oil
* 1 large or 2 small sweet onions, diced
* 3 large carrots, cut into thick disks
* 1 celery stalk, chopped
* 8 cloves of garlic, minced
* 1 28-ounce can diced tomatoes
* 2 (15-ounce) cans cannellini or kidney beans, drained and rinsed
* 1 cup chopped green beans
* 4 cups vegetable broth
* 1–2 teaspoon each dried oregano, thyme, rosemary, and basil
* Bay leaf
* Salt and pepper, to taste
* 1 box (16 ounces) dried small pasta (I use elbows)
* Parmesan cheese to grate on top (omit if vegan)

1. Heat your oil however your crone heart desires. (I make sure my cauldron is hot before adding oil, but I use cast iron or stainless steel. Your technique may vary.) Add onions, carrots and celery and sauté for about 5 to 7 minutes, until onions are translucent.
2. Add garlic, tomatoes, beans, green beans, broth, all herbs, and salt and pepper. Cover and simmer for 20 to 25 minutes.
3. Stir in dried pasta and continue simmering until pasta is cooked through (usually 8 to 10 minutes.)
4. Salt and pepper to taste, then ladle into a bowl and enjoy!

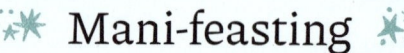

✳ Mani-feasting ✳

What if you can't cook—or just don't want to? "Girl dinner" is a thing for a reason—that's what we're calling snack dinner these days, apparently, though I always considered my "fourteen olives, a handful of dried figs, and cheese cubes (manchego)" meals more "Big Divorcée Energy." Cooking can be fun, but it's still labor. The freedom of being a crone is to say *fuck it* and follow your desires.

Remember how we said spells are all about intention? Nothing turns intention into nourishing reality like ordering takeout.

YOU'LL NEED

* Your phone
* Your preferred food delivery app

THE RITUAL

1. Open your preferred delivery app or the ordering site of your favorite local joint.
2. Create your intention, also known as your food order.
3. Seal your intention by adding a generous tip.
4. Speak aloud the words: "As I am now hungry, so shall I be fed!"
5. Tap ORDER NOW or SUBMIT.
6. Your intention will manifest in thirty to ninety minutes!

Crone Cocktails

When I need to banish the negative energy of a terrible day, or I'm craving a binding ritual with my boyfriend, I turn to the spirits. Also known as cocktails.

Cocktails embody the art of alchemy, requiring all sorts of magical tools: a tall stainless-steel (or glass) receptacle; a wooden wand for muddling; a long, ritual spoon. The mixture is stirred or shaken, then strained over a glass designed for that specific rite. Garnish with a magical herb.

Here are some potent potables to add to your libational grimoire. It's time for crone cocktails! (Not every crone finds alcohol magical, so I've included nonalcoholic adjustments for each of the drinks below.)

CRONEICILLIN

A take on the classic Penicillin cocktail, using muddled fresh ginger instead of ginger syrup.

* 3 slices fresh ginger
* 2 ounces blended whiskey
* ¾ ounce fresh lemon juice
* ¾ ounce honey syrup (2:1 honey to warm water, whisked until syrupy)
* Sprig of fresh basil, for garnish

Muddle ginger slices in a cocktail shaker, then add whiskey, lemon juice, honey syrup, and ice. Shake, then strain over a big rock ice cube in a lowball glass. Garnish with basil sprig. Feel better instantly!

Banishing spirits?
Substitute nonalcoholic whiskey or strong tea for the blended whiskey.

SORCIÈRE 72

An herbaceous take on my favorite cocktail, the French 75.

* 1 ounce gin
* ½ ounce rosemary-infused simple syrup (to make your own, see page 110)
* ½ ounce lemon juice
* Champagne or sparkling wine, to top
* Sprig of fresh thyme, for garnish

Add gin, rosemary syrup, lemon juice, and ice to a cocktail shaker and shake. Pour into a flute glass and top with bubbly. Garnish with thyme sprig. Thank me later.

> **Banishing spirits?**
> Use nonalcoholic sparkling wine instead of champagne.

TOIL AND TROUBLE

This cocktail is based on the Philly Fish House Punch, which dates back to 1732. But while it's nearly three hundred years old, this punch still packs quite a wallop.

* 1½ ounce Jamaican rum
* 1 ounce cognac
* 1 ounce citrus-forward tea, cold
* ¾ ounce fresh grapefruit juice
* ¾ ounce fresh lime juice
* ¾ ounce honey syrup (see page 107)
* 3 dashes of Angostura bitters

- Prosecco (or other sparkling wine), to top
- Grapefruit wedges or lime wheels, for garnish

Add everything except prosecco to a cocktail shaker and shake over ice. Pour into lowball glass over ice, then top with prosecco. Garnish with grapefruit or lime.

Banishing spirits?

Omit the rum and cognac and, if desired, substitute nonalcoholic rum. Top with seltzer instead of prosecco.

DOUBLE, DOUBLE TOIL AND TROUBLE

It's easy to batch the Toil and Trouble cocktail for your coven. Guests can serve themselves out of your cauldron—or your punch bowl.

- 18 ounces (550 mL) Jamaican rum
- 12 ounces cognac
- 9 ounces honey syrup (see page 107)
- 36 dashes Angostura bitters
- 1 bottle (750 mL) prosecco
- 9 ounces grapefruit juice
- 9 ounces lime juice
- 12 ounces citrus-forward tea, cold
- 12 ounces water, chilled
- Grapefruit wheels and lime wheels, for garnish

Combine everything but prosecco, citrus juices, and water in your cauldron (or punch bowl). Add juices and prosecco at the last minute. Stir to combine, then add water and large ice cubes (or a big block of ice). Garnish bowl with grapefruit and lime wheels. Ladle into punch cups.

No cauldron? Combine everything but prosecco and citrus juices in a pitcher. (This can be done ahead of time and stored in the fridge.) Right before the crones arrive, add citrus juices to the pitcher and place an open bottle of prosecco next to it. Guests can then serve themselves.

SPELL IT OUT

Simply Syrups

Making your own simple syrup may feel like Advanced Potion Making, but like its name implies, it's ridiculously simple. Stir equal parts sugar (I like to use superfine sugar, but regular granulated sugar is fine) and water in a saucepan over medium heat until the sugar dissolves completely. Let cool, then pour into a glass container. Your syrup should be stored in the refrigerator, and will stay fresh for about a month.

But if you'd like to up your magic factor, then herbal simple syrups are the potion you're looking for. Infuse the herb whose properties appeal to you, and add a mystical boost to your cocktail—or bubbly water, tea, or juice (mint lemonade, anyone?). You'll just need water, sugar, a saucepan, your chosen herb (either fresh or dried), something to stir and strain with, and a jar to keep it in.

Mint simple syrup: Uplifts mood, promotes mental clarity, relieves stress

Rosemary simple syrup: Cleanses, protects, attracts

Thyme simple syrup: Promotes courage, protection, and healing

HERB-INFUSED SIMPLE SYRUP

1. Bring your water to a boil in a saucepan. (It's a 1:1 ratio, so if you use 1 cup of water here, use 1 cup of sugar in step 4.)
2. When water boils remove pan from heat and add 3–4 sprigs of your fresh herb (see the variation below for dried herbs).
3. Cover with a lid and let steep for 15–20 minutes. Longer is fine, but the herb flavor in your syrup will be stronger. (This part is basically the same as making tea!)
4. Strain the herbs out of the water, then add the sugar.
5. Return the pan to medium heat and cook, stirring gently, until sugar is dissolved.
6. Let the syrup cool, then pour into the apothecary jar of your choice. Store in the refrigerator, but make sure it comes to room temperature before using (like any syrup).

For dried herbs: Put 3–4 tablespoons of the dried herb of your choice in a glass jar. Make the simple syrup according to the method above, then pour over the dried herbs. Let cool slightly, then cover the jar and shake to combine. Let cool completely, then strain through cheesecloth.

Let's Get Familiar

In the fall of 2016, my spouse and I bought a house in Van Nuys, California. The gray house on a dead-end street had been flipped by people who had only a smidgen more real estate knowledge than we had—and we had none. But there was a pool! And a hot tub! And a wall of mirrors in the primary bedroom, making me wonder if the house was haunted by the Ghost of Sex Parties Past.

Which is precisely what I was thinking when I woke up in the early hours of the morning the first week we lived there. Dawn crept through the flat sheets that were taped across the sliding glass doors for privacy. (I hadn't picked out drapes yet.) But then I heard what woke me up. A sound. Rustling? I followed it to the guest bathroom. *Something alive was under the tub.*

My spouse insisted it was the wind. There was no way to get under the house, they had checked. But when I said I was going to do a lap around the house just to see, they followed. We had almost completed a full loop around the house when the victory speech began. "See? I told you—"

But there it was, just past the chimney: a ten-inch-by-ten-inch hole, clearly missing a grate. A lynx point Siamese poked her head out of the hole, looking annoyed. "MEOW."

My spouse didn't want me to feed her. We had a dog who was not fond of cats, and it was an accident waiting to happen. But it ended up being a moot point, as I rarely saw the cat after that. Every few months I'd catch a glimpse. Her ear was tipped, so I knew she was fixed, and she appeared healthy. In an act of marital compromise, I only put out water—but I kept an eye out.

Four years later, I was newly divorced and the world was in the middle of a pandemic. The quiet of the shutdown brought the cat out of hiding. She still looked healthy. But I decided upon my first act of post-divorce defiance. *I was going to feed that goddamned cat.*

At first, she was a ghost. I assumed she was eating the food, because it was gone by the afternoon, but I never saw her. After a few days, she'd watch me from a healthy distance. A week later, she left me a severed rat head next to her bowl as a tip. Three weeks after that, she came right up and let me pet her.

Over the next few years, more stray cats showed up. I went from one, to two, to four. Three had already been fixed, and the fourth—a giant, truly feral tuxedo tomcat—I trapped and had fixed with the help of a friend. The original two are living out their golden years with my old roommate. The third (who needed pricey dental work) lives with her two dads and splits her time between San Francisco and Palm Springs. The formerly feral tuxedo tomcat is currently curled up at the edge of my bed wearing a bow tie.

I've fallen victim to the classic crone curse. You know which curse I'm talking about: **the childless cat lady, old and alone with her seventeen cats.**

The person who invokes this curse thinks they're being clever and biting. But all it does is show their complete ignorance of the crone arts. Because to a crone, this isn't a curse. It's a blessing.

SOUND FAMILIAR?

In folklore, when a crone has a pet cat or black goat or talking crow or what have you, it's probably her familiar—an animal companion (possibly a demon in animal form) who is bound to do her bidding. In real life, this is only partly correct. My formerly feral tuxedo cat (his name is Ron Swanson) *is* frequently a demon. But the only will he carries out is his own. Still, it's fun to think of our pets as our familiars, because we *do* share a kind of magical bond. I can tell Ron Swanson anything! Sure, he doesn't respond or listen or do anything I say. But still, what a team!

Now, you may not just be gifted a feral cat by the universe. You may have to search for your companion animal. And because different crones have different needs, abilities, and budgets, here's a handy quiz to figure out which familiar is right for you.

FIND YOUR FAMILIAR

The word that best describes you is:

A. Independent

B. Outgoing

C. Reclusive

D. Watchful

E. Cursed

You walk into a room of strangers. You:

A. Lurk in the corner.

B. Walk up to a group and introduce yourself.

C. Stay in your shell 'til food arrives.

D. Scream into the void.

E. Hex them all!

Favorite *Twin Peaks* character?

A. Audrey Horne

B. Dale Cooper

C. Harold Smith

D. Log Lady

E. Laura Palmer

You find yourself with a spare hour in your schedule. You:

A. Nap. Life is exhausting.

B. Exercise. It's important to work out that energy.

C. Bask in the sun. Gotta get that vitamin D.

D. Eat. It's always time for snacks.

E. Scroll. Creep the Insta of the girl who bullied you in high school.

Favorite streaming service?

A. BritBox. American TV is so tedious.

B. Netflix. What else is there?

C. Crunchyroll. It even sounds delicious.

D. Shudder. The world is horror.

E. Peacock. No one's more cursed than a Real Housewife.

Who are you in the group project?

A. The one who works solo. You can't trust anyone with your grade.

B. The one who asks for everyone's input. It's important to work as a team.

C. The one who shows up but doesn't say a word. You don't have to be friends with these people.

D. The one who disappears. No one ever bothers the weird kid.

E. The one who shows up with a perfectly executed but wrong assignment. Unpredictability is fun!

What's your preferred level of activity?

A. I'm not lazy, but the less I leave the house, the better.

B. I can't handle sitting still, I need to always do something!

C. A touch more than "none."

D. I like *being* outside but I don't like *doing* anything outside.

E. Paranormal.

RESULTS

Mostly A's: Your perfect familiar is a cat. You're not a complete hermit, you just like to be alone . . . but together. And you don't mind an adorable apex predator living in your house.

Mostly B's: Your perfect familiar is a dog. You're sociable, requiring regular interaction with the outside world. And you want someone who thinks you hung the moon while you both howl at it.

Mostly C's: Your perfect familiar is a turtle. You're not the cuddly sort. You would prefer not to be bothered, but will compromise for a hot stone massage or snacks.

Mostly D's: Your perfect familiar is a murder of crows. You're not looking for a full-time commitment, just some chaos and squawking, along with the occasional shiny gift.

Mostly E's: Your perfect familiar is a haunted doll. *You're in trouble.*

SO YOU WANT TO COMMIT (TO) A MURDER?

I have been nominated for an Emmy, posed for a pinup calendar, and been invited to speak at various institutes of higher learning. But I would toss every single one of those experiences straight into the trash to achieve the one true goal of my life: to have a crow friend bring me a gift. A loyal murder (the collective noun for crows) is every crone's right, and it's easier than it sounds.

Making friends with crows (or any corvids: ravens, jays, magpies, etc.) is not unlike making friends with other crones. (It would certainly work on me.) It breaks down into three simple steps.

* Be patient and nonthreatening. Trust has to be built over time.
* Visit regularly and often. Showing up on the occasional Tuesday isn't going to cut it. Friendship takes work!
* Most importantly: Bring snacks, such as unsalted nuts, hard-boiled eggs, peas, high-quality cat kibble, or hamburger. Double check that what you're feeding is safe! Also, clean your feeding stations regularly—bacteria can grow and make your friends sick if you don't.

That's really all there is to it! On a regular schedule, go to a specific place where you've spotted potential bird friends and leave them some food. Crows are really smart—hence why we're interested in befriending them in the first place—and they'll start to recognize your face. You'll get a sense of what snacks they like best, and they may even start bringing you gifts.

More crow friend tips:

* **Make some noise.** I make a clicking noise when I put out food for wildlife so even if the crows (or squirrels, or rabbits, or chipmunks, or possums) don't see me, they hear me and associate the sound with me—and with being fed.
* **Safety first.** Put the food somewhere that your new friends will be safe while eating. I use both hanging feeders and a tray feeder tucked under a bush or tree so they have some cover from predators.
* **Go public.** Don't entice crow friends to a property you share with close neighbors unless you're absolutely sure your neighbors are cool with it. You may want to choose a public park or green space.
* **Water, water everywhere.** Provide fresh and clean water for the birds to drink and bathe in. Make sure the bowl isn't too deep—I like to use a shallow plant saucer, but you can also add stones to cut down on the depth of the water. Fresh water is especially vital during the winter months in places where the temperature drops below freezing. Heated

birdbaths (that use electrical or solar energy) are the easiest way to prevent the water bowl from turning into an ice bath. An added benefit is that it can quickly become a meetup spot for your local murder. Position the bowl in a place where you can observe your avian friends from the warm embrace of your crone's cottage.

* **Do not invoke their wrath.** Crows remember faces—and that goes for their enemies as well as their benefactors. Don't get on their bad side. (Again: it's not unlike befriending other crones.)

Some treats to try leaving for your corvid friends:

* Unshelled nuts
* Freeze-dried dog treats
* Cat kibble
* Bread, but not too much
* Mealworms
* Cheese slices
* Cooked chicken (cannibalism?)
* Hot dog pieces
* Oats
* Berries
* Grapes
* Figs
* Corn kernels
* Hard-boiled eggs (cannibalism??)

The number-one rule to remember when it comes to befriending crows (or any wildlife) is DO NO HARM. Do not overfeed the animals to the point that they rely on you to be fed. They're still wild animals, and they need to be able to take care of themselves. Make sure that what you're feeding them is safe and appropriate. And be cool—if you make a mess and create a situation where your neighbors complain, you're only putting the crows—and yourself—at risk.

Finally, don't try to force any interactions. Appreciate crows as equals—unbothered, wild, and free. They'll acknowledge you if they want to acknowledge you, on their timeline, and when they're ready.

Because it's not just that crows remember faces. They also share that information with other crows. So if you befriend a crow, you've got a potential crow army in the making. (Crone goals!) But in the spirit of "as above, so below," the flip side is also true. Cross a crow, and you will be crone non grata as they will turn their murder against you. In fact, recent research has suggested that crows hold grudges for up to seventeen years, passing down their animus not only to other crows but to their offspring. Generations of grudge-holding crows, ready to whip up a vengeful murder? Honestly, goals.

Crone Sweet Home

At the beginning of 2023, facing a mountain of postdivorce debt and a writers' strike, I sold my house in Los Angeles and moved back to the Midwest. I'm currently living in the house that I grew up in—in my childhood bedroom, no less. I am beyond grateful that I have a family that is willing to give me a place to land, but even though I'm in a familiar place with familiar people, it doesn't feel like my home. For months, I was stuck in the liminal space between two worlds. Living here, but not really being here. I felt completely unmoored.

The only thing that helped was when I stopped fighting that feeling of being lost, unsettled, and in-between and leaned into the idea of being in transition. I had to access the **Wisdom** to honor my instinctive sense of not being home (even though, in a literal sense, I was home!), my **Knowledge** to understand what I wanted my eventual home to look and feel like, and especially my **Fuck It**—so I could truly say "okay, I'm in a holding pattern, and there's something comforting and beautiful about that." Crones love dwelling outside of expectations, in wild areas like forests and bogs. Why shouldn't I feel just as comfortable in my liminal space?

With that, I found ways to make this liminal space mine. To tether myself to my current circumstances, but also give myself enough freedom to think about how to make the next space a reality. Each thought became inspiration for this chapter: My familiar, Ron Swanson (the cat). My painting of Daisy J. Dog. My herb garden, my wildlife feeding stations, my haunted bed linens, my chicken soup, my cocktails, my crow friends. I began to think of myself as my own home.

It's my hope that you're currently reading this curled up in your comfiest chair in the witch's cottage of your dreams. But if that's not your reality, please know that you're not alone. You may feel untethered, but this is me throwing you a rope and reminding you that what makes a crone home is you.

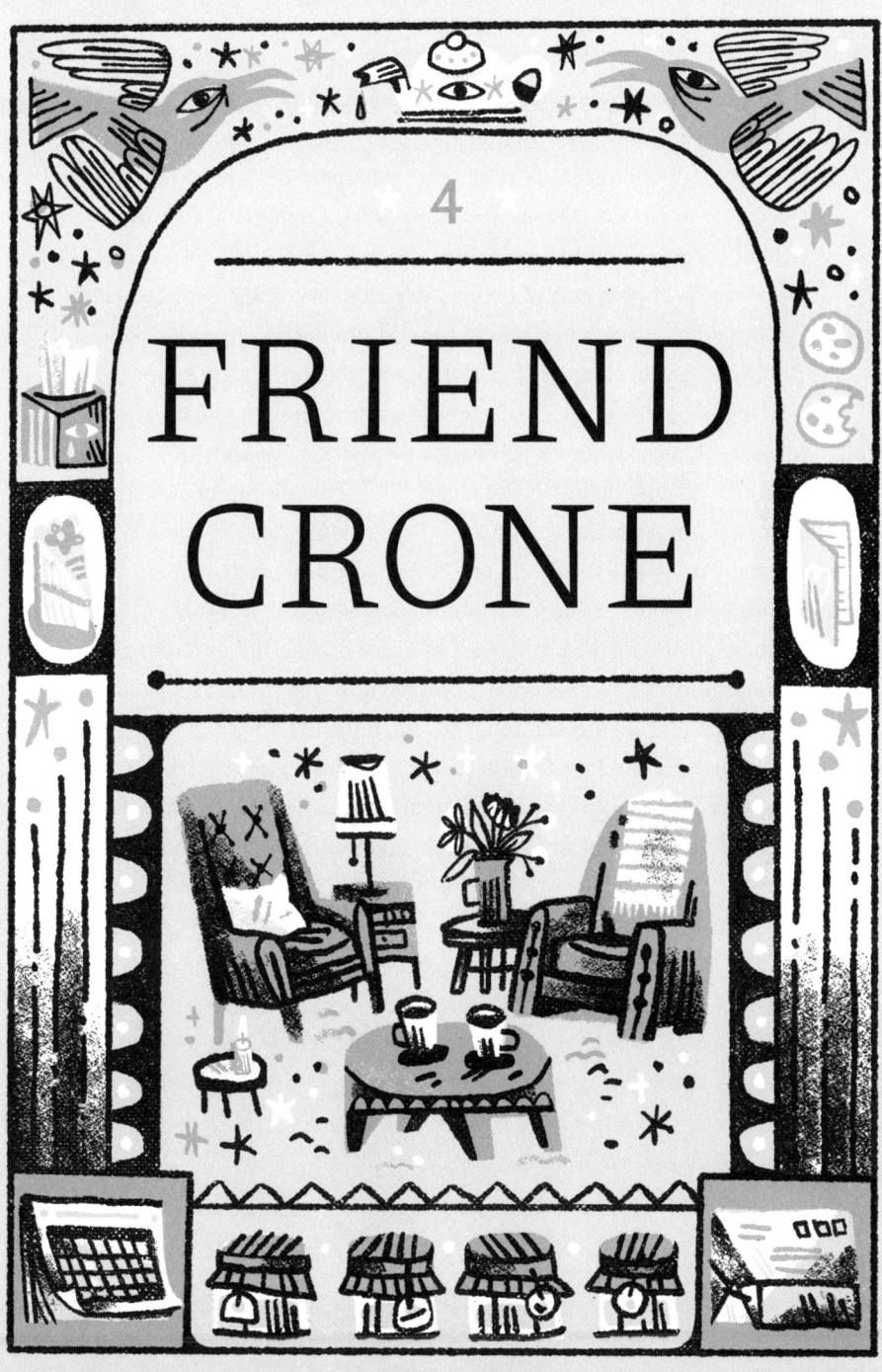

4

FRIEND CRONE

The archetypal crone is usually portrayed as a solitary figure, a hermit, an outcast. Her crabby countenance doesn't exactly invite intimacy, or call out for companionship. But the crone has spent her life taking care of everyone else in her life. Maybe she wants to have a moment free from responsibility, from attending to everyone else's needs.

Of course, we're big fans of defying expectations, refusing to be useful, and prioritizing our own needs for a change! But friends aren't people who need stuff from you—they're an essential part of looking after yourself. I'm not talking about "friends," like the woman who bullied you all through middle school and now sends you Facebook invites to "a once-in-a-lifetime opportunity" that is "definitely not an MLM!!!!" I'm talking about your own Golden Girls, or Witches of Eastwick, or Sanderson sisters—people with whom you can let the mask slip and reveal yourself, warts and all. These relationships are the beating heart of our crone years.

Friends are the load-bearing wall of every crone's life, providing support, community, and connection as we navigate the peaks and valleys of our crone era. Having a coven to laugh, cry, or just talk with can be a cozy blanket in an often cold world. So whether you find friendship an easy road to navigate or, like me, you're a T. rex stumbling through a minefield of awkwardness, it's time to look at the magical nature of crone friendship.

IN THIS CHAPTER, WE'LL LEARN:

* How get vulnerable by breaking through your hard candy shell
* How to reconnect when your friends have disappeared
* Ways to commune with your coven
* The benefit of inviting younger witches into your friendship circles
* How to let a friendship go
* How to deal with jealousy and resentment

The Hard Candy Shell

If you're a woman, or if other people sometimes see you as a woman, you're probably used to being treated like public property. Sometimes it feels like no matter where you are, how you're dressed, or how many pairs of giant headphones you wear, someone's always trying to get in your business.

It can be harmless but annoying, like when you're listening to a podcast on the train and Business Brad wants to chitchat. Or downright terrifying, like when you're trying to take a walk and a car full of men follows you. We begin to don armor before heading out into the world in an attempt to be left alone. We wear headphones, carry books, hold our keys as weapons, or pretend to be on the phone. Honestly, resting bitch face is probably an evolutionary reaction to being bothered every time we leave the house.

We get so used to having to protect ourselves from the world that it becomes second nature—even once we hit cronehood and gain our invisibility superpower. Armor isn't something we think about anymore. It's a part of us now, a permanent exoskeleton, the hard candy shell that protects our gooey emotional center.

But our gooey emotional center is where all the good stuff is: our hopes and dreams and fears and anxieties, the things we love and the things we hate, the things we're ashamed of or embarrassed by. And that's where friendship begins. A hairline crack in that hard shell—a moment of connection, of honesty, of letting someone see *you*—allows the first seeds of friendship to take root. And in order for that friendship to grow, your shell needs to remain cracked open and vulnerable.

Thanks to therapy (which I didn't start until after reaching cronedom), I've learned that the reason I always had such a difficult time making friends is that I was (am) terrified of being vulnerable. It's much easier to build layer upon layer of that hard shell than actually let people see what's inside. There are reasons the shell is so thick.

But I've also discovered that feeling protected doesn't have to mean being isolated. There's comfort and companionship to be found within our crone communities if you just take the chance. There's power, too! The world barely knows how to handle one crone. Imagine how it will react to an entire coven.

Part of cracking that hard candy shell is getting comfortable with the gooey stuff inside. Don't worry, I'm not going to ask you to drop your cloak and parade around emotionally naked for the whole world to see. Consider baring an ankle of intimacy. Dip a toe into the touchy-feely waters. Or, to paraphrase the sage wisdom of *The Real World*: stop being polite and start getting real.

 SPELL IT OUT

Cracking the Hard Candy Shell

The intention of this spell is to get comfy with—or at least get used to— the emotional parts of yourself. Your gooey emotional center may contain the things you hide due to embarrassment or shame, but it also holds your secret dreams and small joys. So let's make friends with all of it. And what's the first step to making friends? Learn their names!

YOU'LL NEED

* A large piece of paper (you may want to use wrapping paper or a paper shopping bag for the generous surface area)
* A bag of candies with a shell and a softer center—M&M's, Reese's Pieces, Rolos, etc. The size of the bag is up to you.
* A marker or pen

1. Lay your paper out on a flat surface.

2. Close your eyes, take a deep breath, and dig down into your gooey center. What are the hopes, dreams, or anxieties in there that you feel scared to share? Maybe it's bizarre, but harmless ("I obsessively study bee dancing"). Or a perceived personal failure ("I got so in my head that I bailed on my mom's seventy-second birthday party").

3. Write each of these thoughts down on the paper, then place a piece of candy next to each thought.

4. Claim an issue by speaking it aloud ("I love bee dancing and I don't care who knows it!" "I don't love that I bail, but sometimes I have to!") Then press your thumb down on the candy until the shell ruptures. Repeat with each issue/candy.

5. Eat as much of the leftover candy as you like while you observe the remnants of your fears before you.

6. Optional: Snap a photo of your issues (and your decimated candy) and print it out for your grimoire.

Coven Love

No matter how much everyone professes to love *The Golden Girls*, the world isn't exactly putting out the welcome mat for crones. First, they'd have to see us. Then, they'd have to acknowledge us as human beings. And then they'd ask us where the welcome mat is, even though they used it last.

You know who understands being treated this way? Your fellow crones.

Our crone communities can be places of comfort, sources of strength, and forces of nature. They understand the fury boiling in our blood—and they can recommend an herb to help with that. Who cares if other people see us? What's important is that we see each other. And if we continue to build our community, one day the world may be forced to see us. Not in a world domination way, that seems exhausting—I'm talking in an "acknowledging our existence as humans" kind of way. Although maybe also world domination? I'm pretty sure I could assemble an army of crows to do my bidding. Forget girl power. It's all about crone conspiracy!

Girl power: Infantilizing, trite, commodified
Crone conspiracy: Devious, sexy, confusing to outsiders

COMMUNING WITH YOUR COVEN

Even if we wanted to perform a mass spell to transform society, how could we do it when we can barely find forty-five minutes to grab coffee? Making time to see friends has a tendency to find its way to the bottom of our to-do list.

I've found that hangouts are more likely to happen if they're planned around an activity—especially if everyone in the coven is involved in the planning. (Sometimes the planning becomes the hangout itself.) So here are some suggestions for communing with your coven. Mix and match, use them as a jumping off point, or create your own! (And let me know how it turned out.)

FIEND-SHIP BRACELETS

Everyone knows witches love to cast a circle. Bracelet-making gives you the chance to cast a physical one. Even the most beginner crafter can make bracelets. Jewelry-making kits make it even easier. Create bracelets for your fellow crones, imbuing them with a specific intention or message—deciding on this together is the most fun part! If you do this as a coven, pair off so everyone makes and receives a bracelet.

Options include:

* **Runes:** Use letter beads to spell out your invocation or intent.
* **Crystals:** Use crystal beads according to their meaning (calming, healing, attracting, etc.) to create a bracelet that evokes a certain vibe.
* **Charmed charms:** Find (or make) charms that symbolize the wearer, and use them to create a bracelet that acts as a talisman.

CAULDRON OF COMFORT

Invite your coven over for a giant vat of soup. If this sounds ridiculous to you, just try it. Soup is easy to make, a cost-effective way to feed a crowd, and the closest thing we have to a healing potion. Plus it's low-key. Show up in your PJs and no bra. Soup is here for you! (If you're looking for a recipe, my chicken soup on page 103 is time-tested and coven-approved.)

WITCHES' BREW

Crone-source your cocktail party! Use your powers of alchemy to create a signature cocktail, and have your coven-mates bring nibbles. It's easy to batch cocktails: mix the nonalcoholic ingredients in a pitcher, then add spirits to individual glasses when serving. Alternatively, get out your big cauldron and make a punch so guests can serve themselves. (Don't forget to have a nonalcoholic version for witches who don't imbibe!) Check out the crone cocktails on page 107 to get started.

TEAPOTLUCK

Host a crone-sourced tea party, where each guest brings a tiny bite and a tea to try. This kind of gathering is perfect for foggy days in the bog or chilly forest nights. Make sure you have plenty of teapots, steepers, and charming little teacups (or big honking mugs) on hand. If you want to add an activity, why not learn to read tea leaves?

THE TRAVELING MARKET OF CURSED OBJECTS

We've all lived long enough to accumulate something that we feel like we can't donate or throw away. Your ex-girlfriend's old guitar. Your Great-Aunt Peggy's collection of clown dolls. Your wedding album. Gather your coven to exchange your cursed items! After all, the items are only cursed to you, so your friends won't have any problems getting rid of them. Except for Great-Aunt Peggy's clown dolls. For some reason, those keep showing back up.

GET CARDED

Need to download to your friends but don't know where to begin? Tarot readings to the rescue! This activity is perfect for crowded covens or a couple of crones. Sit in a circle (if there's a bunch of you) or across from each other (if there's just a few). Pull a card from the deck. Use the meaning behind whatever card you've pulled to discuss what's happening in your life. Not super familiar with tarot or don't own a deck? Use one of the many tarot apps or resources online.

Magic Words for the Modern Crone

Here are a few tips that have strengthened all my friendships, as well as words to say when you don't know what to say.

* **Sympathy or suggestions?** When a friend shares a terrible story about their day (in person or online), it can be tempting to want to offer advice immediately. (So, so tempting.) But when you offer unsolicited advice, it

can feel like a judgment or a pile-on. If you're not sure what to do, just ask: "What do you need from me right now?"

* **Let *them* know.** When a friend is going through it, we all say "Let me know if you need anything." But they never let you know, because it feels weird to ask. Especially when it comes to the small day-to-day stuff. Make a specific suggestion: "You probably haven't had time to do laundry, can I do it for you?" Or "I'd like to order dinner for you—what can I send over?" (You can use the spell on page 106 to imbue the food with a little extra intention.)

* **Sit in the muck.** Sometimes there are no magic words when your friend has experienced a huge loss. You can't fix it. But you can sit with them through it.

The Golden Girls

You can't write about crone friendship and not mention *The Golden Girls*. The show, created by Susan Harris in 1985, ran on NBC for seven seasons, spawned a spin-off (*The Golden Palace*), and has become the symbol of female friendship. You probably even started singing the show's iconic theme song, "Thank You for Being a Friend," the second you read the title.

The show is about four older women living out their "golden years" together in a house in Miami. I don't imagine any of these women thought their life would turn out this way. After all, marriage is one of the ways to ward off the solitary nature of cronedom. But Blanche (Rue McClanahan) and Rose (Betty White) were both widowed. Dorothy's (Bea Arthur) husband of thirty-eight years had an affair, then served her divorce papers. Then Dorothy's mom, Sophia (Estelle Getty), had to move in when her retirement home burned down.

Each character embodied the best of cronedom or turned it on its ear. Man-hungry Blanche proved that sex doesn't stop at forty. Rose's folksy stories about growing up in St. Olaf, Minnesota, had their own peculiar sort of wisdom. Sophia's ability to cut through the bullshit is a star crone talent. And Dorothy's caustic wit and savage takedowns of only the most deserving? No notes. It's everything I want a crone to be.

The Golden Girls is a TV show. But it can be a harbinger of what can happen when we seek out community and forge friendships with fellow crones. Cronedom isn't the end. It's only the beginning.

Ch-Ch-Ch-Changes

In my twenties, Friday nights were spent playing answering-machine tag with my friends, figuring out where we were going, who was driving, and was there enough room in my bra to hold everyone's ID? We'd go from goth club to karaoke bar to cocktail lounge, finally ending up at a late-night diner where we'd feast on plates of corned beef hash or bowls of matzo ball soup.

There were fewer late-night drunken pastrami runs in my thirties. We were all too busy with our careers, relationships, or a combo pack. Friends got engaged, got married, got promoted, changed careers, had children, moved away. Time and energy that once seemed limitless were now finite commodities to be traded on the "adult with responsibilities" stock exchange.

The rules governing our outings changed drastically. Barhopping was no more. Epic evenings were limited to single locations. And *epic* meant three hours, tops. No one wanted to waste time looking for parking, so there had to be a lot or valet, and, finally, no more accepting drugs in the bathroom from strangers. (Okay, that last one was a rule I made for myself.) Finally, we promised at the end of every get-together to "do this more often!" Spoiler alert: we never did.

Eventually, those friendships fizzled out. There were no petty slights or giant arguments leading to one final pronouncement that *the friendship was over*! We just got busy. And since it was the early aughts, social media didn't exist in the way it does now. Those relationships were put in a box, like Schrödinger's friendship: neither alive nor dead, neither friends nor not friends.

Friendships drift off even when you're connected by social media. You get busy and don't check in. The algorithm stops showing you their posts. You mute them by mistake. (Or you mute them on purpose because they're on a two-week road trip and they post twenty-three photos of every hotel room they stay in, *even though every Days Inn looks exactly the same, Alice*).

Then one day they pop up in your feed. But their preschooler is now a high schooler and the road trip is now a college tour. The Days Inn, however, looks exactly the same.

As you enter your crone era, you may find yourself wanting to revisit those ghosts of friendships past. Whether it's curiosity or a desire to truly reconnect, here are some handy guidelines for conjuring pals from the past!

SET INTENTIONS

Every spell begins with an intention. And while this isn't a spell per se, we are summoning the spirit of our past. Investigating what our motives are can save you (and the other person) from confusion or disappointment later.

* **Nosy:** You want to know how their life turned out, but you have zero plans to reach out.
* **Curious:** You want to know how their life turned out, and you might reach out depending on what you find.
* **Committed:** It doesn't matter what you find; this witch is definitely getting a DM.

CURIOUSER AND CURIOUSER

Before you reach out, snoop the friend's socials. The longer you've been out of contact, the further back you should look. You don't need to scroll through ten years of their Insta posts, but go beyond the first few rows of their grid. Don't be like me, who discovered an old friend's husband had dumped her publicly on Facebook *after* I sent the email that ended with "I hope Brad is great!!!"

Things to know before you scroll:

* The further back you scroll, the more careful you should be not to accidentally "like" something.

* Know that some sites (like LinkedIn) will show them that you peeked at their profile!
* If the person is not on social media, it's totally acceptable to inquire about them with a trusted mutual friend. Just be aware that information from a third party might be a little dicier. Your former friend may be hurt that you went through a mutual friend rather than asking them directly. To them, it may end up feeling like an invasion of privacy.

Now the big question: do you want to summon the past?

MANAGE EXPECTATIONS

So you've decided to summon the ghost of friendship past. Know that whatever you put out into the universe may not be what you receive back. Here are some magic words for managing your expectations when it comes to a response.

BRIDGES AND BOUNDARIES

* I'm not committing to anything by reaching out. I can check in without becoming besties again!
* I am realistic about the time and effort I want to devote to rebuilding this friendship.

THE SPELL OF TRANSFORMATION

* We remember old friends as we last saw them, so they become frozen in our minds as they were. But they may not be those people now.
* I can meet my former friend where they are, but I am not obligated to like them just because we were once friends. I can always close the book and walk away.

THE SPELL OF FORGETTING

* Time has a way of softening the edges of our memory, and nostalgia for the past can cloud our judgment. I will not look for problems that aren't there, but I will make sure my vision is clear.

THE CURSE OF TIME TRAVEL

* Bringing something from the past into the present can have unforeseen consequences. I will approach this trip into the past with my eyes open.

FRIENDSHIP ALCHEMY

What if you reached out and it went terribly? Your friend was furious about some slight that you were completely unaware of? (Happened to me.) Or you reconnected and it felt like you were rebuilding a real friendship and then they ghosted you? (Also happened to me.) Or they didn't respond at all? (Hasn't happened to me but only due to lack of trying.)

There's a certain alchemy to friendships that can't always be replicated. If summoning the ghost of friendships past didn't work out how you wanted, then return to your first two crone touchstones: the **Wisdom** of knowing who you are and the **Knowledge** of understanding what you want. Perhaps this was a friendship that could only exist in that unique time. Perhaps the ways you—or the other person—have changed make a current relationship untenable. Perhaps you're reminded of why you stopped being friends in the first place. (This sort of introspective work is excellent to record in your grimoire!)

Even if it's obvious that the friendship didn't have the required alchemy to survive the present day, this realization may sting a little bit. That's totally normal. Hopefully, you can get to **Fuck It** quickly. Take it on your warty chin, extend the person grace (or don't think of them at all), and move on. You now have room in your relationship garden for other friendships to grow!

Maidens and Mothers

Most of what we've discussed thus far in this chapter has concerned our friendships with fellow crones. But we've yet to discuss the value of communing with witches of all ages—especially those who are younger than you. You may think you have zero in common with anyone under twenty-five . . . okay, maybe thirty-five. Maybe forty. And that's the point. While we have age and experience on our side, younger people have their own unique wisdom to share. Developing connections across age lines keeps a crone's heart soft and her brain open to acknowledging different experiences and points of view. It can also keep us curious. (Plus, they can tell you who everyone is at the Grammys.)

BUBBLE, BUBBLE . . .

Unless you're a crone who's surrendered to the quiet, internet-free life in the damp bog (jealous!), you're probably familiar with the term *living in a bubble*. But for the bog witches amongst us, living in a bubble is when we surround ourselves with people who are just like us. It causes a sort of groupthink mentality, in which those living inside the bubble cannot imagine, much less acknowledge, anyone outside it. The bubble creates not only a lack of empathy but a void of curiosity.

I would never suggest that *you* lack curiosity or empathy. However, we're all creatures of habit, clinging to the things we find most familiar. We can even stay in our crone bubble as long as we acknowledge that we're in it and remain open to what else is out there in the overflowing bath of humanity. Obviously, you're under no obligation to be open to people who deny your agency, humanity, or right to exist. But don't ignore the potential for connection with people whose difference is a matter of circumstance—like, say, people a lot younger than you. Getting to know them can help keep you open-minded, flexible, and up on all the latest memes.

Making it to our crone era is an achievement in and of itself, and I recommend throwing yourself as many parties as you can. Birthdays are still in front of us, but the big rites of passage, the weddings and graduations and bat mitzvahs, are (mostly) behind us. I once lamented to my friend Patty that it was kind of a bummer to think I wouldn't get to celebrate my next big rite of passage.

"Why not?" she asked.

"Because it's my funeral, and I'll be dead."

Having younger witches in your circle allows you the opportunity to be a part of those rites of passage—especially nice for crones with smaller families, or who aren't mothers, aunts, or honorary aunts.

Befriending younger people also helps keep your crone spirit in touch with who you used to be. My (younger) friend Bridget and I were watching a playlist of George Michael videos shortly after he died. At some point, the playlist ended and the algorithm began to select videos at random. And that is when the classic video for David Bowie and Mick Jagger's cover of "Dancing in the Street" appeared on my television screen. When Bridget confessed she had never seen it, I insisted we stop everything and watch.

"Dancing in the Street" was one of my absolute favorite music videos in middle school. But in an objective sense, it's a little bit of a mess. Mick Jagger wears a puffy turquoise shirt and bobs up and down like a life-size jack-in-the-box. Bowie wears a trench coat over an animal-print jumpsuit and dances like a marionette, stiff and jerky. The whole production looks like someone dumped out a pile of cocaine or money (or both) and said, "You have four hours, do whatever." Watching it again as an adult, my excitement turned to confusion. "I'm not sure why I liked this so much?" I told Bridget, embarrassed by my previous enthusiasm.

But Bridget had no such questions. "Oh, no, this explains so much about you," she told me. She rewound the video, freezing on a frame of Bowie and

Jagger dancing face-to-face. "That right there? That's a Nina magnet."

She was right! This 1980s black-box-theater fever dream was the foundation of my entire sexuality. (Were they going to kiss? Did I want them to kiss??) As a Gen X crone, this video was just the backdrop of my younger years. It took watching with someone who didn't grow up around the same time to see it. Sharing one of my cultural touchstones with someone who was raised in a different context helped me understand myself better.

Being part of a different generation than your friends doesn't mean that you can't find real points of connection. The music changes, the fashion changes, the technology changes, but feelings? Feelings are evergreen.

LET'S TALK ABOUT THE CRONE IN THE ROOM

It can be odd being the only person at the party who gets AARP mailers. And it can be hard not to compare yourself to everyone else when you're surrounded by a group of younger friends. But I find that the need to compare rarely comes from the other women. It comes from me. They're not thinking about how old I am—I'm thinking about how young they are. (And, thanks to being surrounded by physical manifestations of the passage of time and the headlong rush toward mortality, I'm also thinking about how old I am.)

Staying on this dark road of comparison can lead straight into the thicket of competition. Even if you don't want it to! It *is* the Magic Mirror's primary message (you remember the Magic Mirror from Chapter 1)—and it's one we've been hearing since birth. *There can be only one fairest one of all, Queen. And Snow White has entered the chat.* Society already loves to pit women against each other. Don't do the work for it.

The other big issue that can befall an age gap friendship is falling into a parent-child dynamic. Do I dream of young women commenting "mother" on my Instagram in that worshipful, I-wanna-be-you-when-I-grow-up kind of way? Of course! But that doesn't mean I actually want to act like their mom. Some things to look out for:

- ✳ **Wait for the ask.** As mentioned on page 128, no matter how wise you are, it's best not to offer advice that hasn't been asked for. Unsolicited advice, even when it's right, can end up feeling like a lecture.
- ✳ **They can go their own way.** Even if your younger friend did ask for guidance? They're not obligated to follow it.
- ✳ **Don't be a hug machine.** On the flip side, if you give good advice and they listen, you risk being used solely as a source of support. Make sure that your friendship is a two-way street.
- ✳ **Young people have wisdom, too.** Make sure you listen as much as you talk.

You might have heard the phrase "As above, so below." It's the Hermetic principle of correspondence: that different planes of existence are connected and work in harmony with each other. And it's what every old crone–young maiden friendship has the potential to be.

The Changing Friend Circle

Friend breakups in your crone era can feel soul-shattering. Losing longtime friends means losing a connection to the past, the person who knew you before you entered cronedom. If your "ride or die" didn't ride or die, you've lost not only them but a little part of *yourself*—the long-ago version of you they witnessed and remember. Even if it wasn't a super-long friendship, losing a friend can really hollow you out. The home that they made in your heart is now empty—but it's not like you can just let someone new move in! Healing takes time. Trust takes time. Creating that easy familiarity that comes with companionship takes time. And as crones, we're aware that our time is beginning to run out.

Which is why it's more important than ever to use the freedom our crone era affords to be unapologetic in our needs and desires—including what we desire from our friendships. Sometimes we've been friends with someone for so long that we don't notice how the friendship has changed. We mistake how long we've known them for how deep our bond is. That doesn't mean you should break up with these friends! You're just figuring out where you want to focus your energies in the second half of your life.

Years ago, some close friends of mine were renting a house for the weekend. The house slept eighteen people. They called me the day before to ask if I wanted to join. A last-minute trip? No, they told me, it had been planned for a while, but people had dropped out. They were in my inner friendship circle. I hadn't made their top eighteen.

Just because you consider someone part of your inner circle doesn't mean they look at you the same way. But learning this can feel like a rejection that's been sitting out in public, waiting for you to notice. It's an awkward position to be in. There is no betrayal to point at, no argument to be had. It's not really a miscommunication but a misunderstanding, and your only option is to accept the friendship as it is or pull away. I didn't end my friendship with the vacation rental people, but I let go of what I thought it was.

SPELL IT OUT

✳ Set Your Story Free ✳

There are numerous rituals to mark the end of romantic relationships, but there are far fewer that mark the end of platonic ones. The goal of this spell is to adjust to the idea of losing someone who holds so much of our personal lore. And we're going to do that by releasing that lore into the world. Use this spell for a friendship that's broken up or fizzled out, or that just needs to be released in some way. Here's a chance to free up space in your library and in your heart!

YOU'LL NEED

* A quiet place to think
* A book you're willing to donate. If you have a plethora of books to choose from, try to select one that reminds you of the friendship that you want to release.
* A pen
* Notecards

THE RITUAL

1. Find somewhere to curl up with your book. It doesn't matter where as long as it feels calm and comforting.
2. Meditate on the friendship you're letting go of. Remember not only how you met the person, but how you bonded. Try to picture a time when you felt the most love for them.
3. Using your notecards, write down a memory or a story about your friendship.
4. Tuck the notecard(s) in the book, saying aloud, "[*Friend's name*], I wish you the best in finishing your story."
5. Donate the book to whatever organization you choose!

Your Crone Worst Enemy

As a young woman, I dated someone for a few months who was a successful TV writer. They had even recently sold a TV show and were still flying high from the sense of accomplishment. But one day they showed up to a date, clearly deflated. When I asked what was wrong, they responded that a friend of theirs had also just sold a TV show. That deal was for millions of dollars. I didn't understand the problem. They both had sold a TV show. They were already in rarefied space. "Yeah," my date responded, "but I didn't sell my show for millions of dollars."

We're supposed to be happy for our friends. But when the gremlin of jealousy comes knocking at our door, it can be difficult not to answer. We're wise enough to know that envy and resentment say more about the envier than they do about the envied—if other people have a problem with *our* success, that's on them. But in this case, that makes things feel worse! It's not enough that I'm jealous of my friends, but now I'm also a terrible, bitter crone who's still jealous of my friends! Great! Perfect! Problem solved.

It's true that if you indulge and feed your jealousy, it can poison your entire life. One day, you see on your friend's LinkedIn that they got a job that you applied for, and the next thing you know, you're a skin suit filled with gremlins. However:

* Being jealous doesn't make you a bad person.
* Being jealous doesn't mean you want something bad to happen.
* Being jealous doesn't mean *that you're not right.*

Maybe you *do* deserve that job or award or fun experience or cool dog! (Maybe you even deserve it more than your friend, though dwelling on that is probably what's going to make you feel bad.) Sometimes envy is the signal that alerts you to your own dreams and ambitions and spurs you to go after them. Even at our big age, it can be hard to admit to ourselves what we really want—especially if you've been told that it's impolite or deluded or unladylike to aim that high. But once we get that signal, we have the **Wisdom** and **Knowledge** to go for it.

Then again, sometimes envy is a clue that the deck *is* stacked against you. And you might be right about that, too! As a television writer, I see people get jobs that they don't deserve all the time, or jobs that I would be much better suited for. The entertainment business is a game of musical chairs, and when you're a crone? There are fewer and fewer places to sit.

So it's good to be able to learn from your jealousy—but it's also good to know when to stop dwelling and just say **Fuck It**. Personally, I try to avoid feelings of envy at all costs. If I feel the hot breath of that gremlin breathing down my neck, I don't ask him how he is, or how his day is going. *I elbow him in his stupid gremlin face.*

THE CRONE METHOD

In my crone era, I've discovered that jealousy becomes a problem only when I let it fester. If I can stop it in its tracks, interrupt the thought pattern that allows it to take hold, it can magically disappear. So if you feel the gremlin of jealousy lurk behind you, use the CRONE method to elbow him in the face:

* **Cease.** Whatever you're doing (unless you're driving or performing surgery), stop. Stop scrolling social media, click on a different browser tab, change the channel.
* **Remove.** Remove yourself from the situation—physically get up from the computer, or if you're with people, pop into a restroom. The mere act of moving can jostle that gremlin loose.
* **Om.** Deep breathing is a quick way to re-center our thoughts.
* **Nature.** People are fond of telling others online to "touch grass," but it really works. Hike, visit a park, or feed the crows.
* **Exorcize.** If nothing has worked and the gremlin has sunk his razor-sharp claws into your chest? It's time for an exorcism. Get those feelings out in whatever way works for you—shouting, journaling, lifting weights, even bitching to other friends.

⁂ Bottle Those Feelings! ⁑

Bottling up your feelings is typically not recommended. But we're not repressing our feelings of bitterness, envy, or animosity. We're bottling up the feelings of success and abundance that we'd like to feel about ourselves and saving them in a spell jar. If you're the kind of crone that I am, your cabinets are already stuffed with an assortment of glass jars you couldn't bear to throw away. Let's put those jars to work.

YOU'LL NEED

* Dried herbs
    * Bay leaf, for writing your intention
    * Basil, for abundance
    * Cinnamon, for prosperity
    * Mint, for wealth and to strengthen the spell
* A glass jar, with or without a lid
* Optional "abundance" items like a lucky penny, an old paycheck, or even a lottery ticket
* Your alone space
* A Sharpie or other marker

THE RITUAL

1. Gather your elements.
2. Write your intention on the bay leaf. It can be specific ("I want to sell a book called *The Crone Zone*") or general ("may I be blessed with career success and financial abundance"). Just remember what you wrote!

3. Add the bay leaf, other herbs, and any abundance items to the jar.

4. Holding the jar, state your intention aloud, then inhale the scent of the fragrant herbs. Imagine abundance flowing through your body.

5. Screw the cap or lid into the jar (if you're using one). Place the abundance jar in a place where abundance may grow: on your desk, next to your computer, in a purse, alongside a checkbook, etc.

6. If the jar is sealed, you can always re-up your intention by speaking it aloud and giving the jar a gentle shake.

7. If your jar is open, continue to add items (more herbs, lucky pennies, etc.) as the mood strikes.

HEX, NO

But what about hexing people? Isn't that an option for dealing with jealousy? I mean, sure. Serious witches and anyone with a solid moral compass will tell you that hexing is bad because it concentrates your energy on negativity or because it will rebound on you tenfold, but I'm not anti-hexing because I'm a good person. I'm anti-hexing because I am lazy. Hexing takes energy. Summoning abundance requires much less energy. Friends, I am a crone. I am exhausted.

So I validate your desire to hex people, but I assure you that they're not worth the effort. If you truly want to hex someone, ask why you're spending any energy on this friendship at all. Your crone years are for real friends. If this person doesn't qualify, cut 'em loose. When I find myself in this situation, I whisper this simple blessing into the wind:

May you get everything you deserve.

They usually do.

Best Fiends Forever

I've forged some of the deepest friendships of my life in my crone years—friends who encourage me to be my full self. Crones aren't afraid of the mess. We've spent decades picking up after everyone else. Finally we have the chance to drop our masks on the floor and make a mess of our own. My wish for you is that you find crone friends and keep them close. Who else understands our rage and frustration, our joys and delights? Our crone friends are there to listen, to comfort, to cheer us on. And, if we need it, to take our hand so we don't have to walk alone into the dark woods.

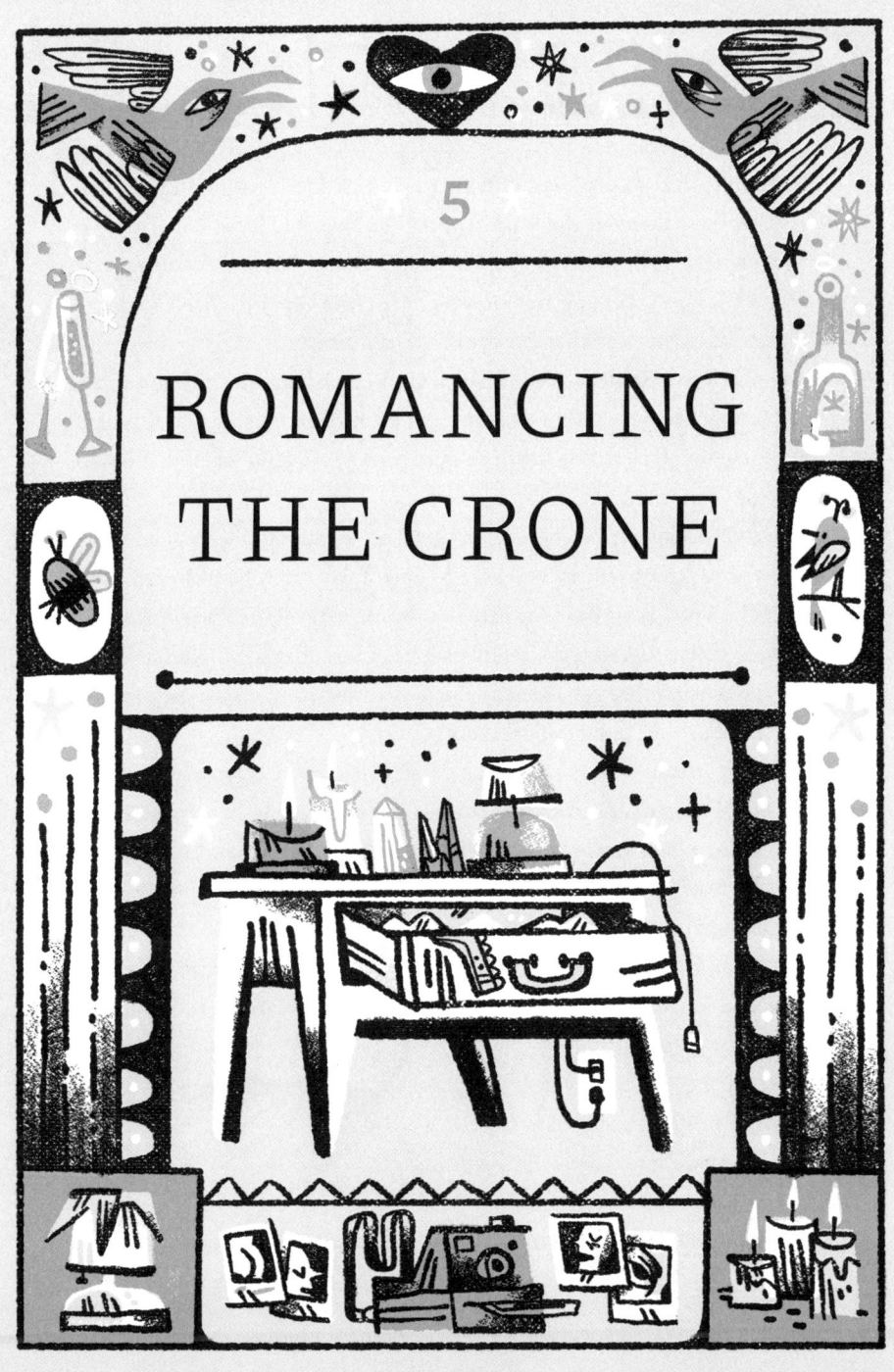

5

ROMANCING
THE CRONE

The classic crone is never sexy. Alas, her days of love and lust are long gone. The ravages of time have rendered her a withered husk, drained of desirability. Her allure has suddenly turned to dust, coating the tumbleweeds that blow through the wasteland of her love life. She is left with two distinct choices: to be of service to her village (Strega Nona) or to disappear into the dark forest, cursing anyone who dare cross her path (Baba Yaga).

If that were true, this chapter would end right here.

The one lesson that has been drilled into our brains since time immemorial is that women have a sexual expiration date. Our desirability is a ticking time bomb counting down to our crone years. And when that bomb detonates? *Game over.*

(This is especially true when it comes to the sexual interests of men—our culture encourages them to be weirdly, dare I say creepily, obsessed with youth. But it's not like crones who are into women are off the hook. For starters, unless you're vigilant, it's really easy to internalize all these messages and start believing that you are fundamentally washed-up past a certain age, no matter what your potential partners believe.)

With our romantic lives retired, the only thing thrust upon us from now on is a life of chastity. Even coupled crones are assumed to live a postsexual existence, their relationships measured by length rather than by affection. For single crones, it's even worse. A crone's solitude is used as evidence that no one desires her. After all, if someone wanted her, she wouldn't be alone! But, my friends, that's just another fairy tale. A crone's solitude isn't proof that she's no longer desired. *A crone's solitude is proof that she has begun to put her desire first.*

By rendering crones invisible, undesirable, and unfuckable, society has unwittingly released us to roam free.

The expectation to couple up? *Poof!* Gone.

The expectation to have children? *Poof!* Gone.

The expectation to stay in a partnership that isn't working, or to restrict ourselves to partnerships that follow all the expected norms and are easy to understand? *Poof!* Gone.

Our concern about what the world thinks of us? *Poof!* Gone.

After spending the last several decades neck deep in the business of life, family, and career, your crone era is finally the time to attend to the business of *you*. So let's get down to business. Strap in or strap on, as we talk about love, sex, divorce, and everything in between.

IN THIS CHAPTER, WE'LL LEARN:

* How to reframe being single and dating in our crone era
* How to summon our sexual selves—or put them to bed
* How to assess our relationships—and decide if we still want one
* How to return to the dating world after a long break

A Single Thing Before We Begin ...

When I began writing this chapter, my plan was to start by discussing married crones. (Or crones in long-term partnerships. Which I'm going to refer to as *married*, not because I'm your Great-Aunt Edna trying to shame your union, but because it's shorter.) I just assumed that most of us hovering around or deep in our crone era are married, so why not start that way?

But single crones always seem to be getting shafted. (And not in the sexy way.) If they're the focus of media, it's as a harbinger or a warning: WOMEN OVER 40 MORE LIKELY TO SPONTANEOUSLY COMBUST THAN MARRY!!! When you travel, everything is based on double occupancy. Even well-intentioned friends can treat single crones as an afterthought (or seat you next to Uncle Roy, who keeps asking about your "boyfriend" while directing all questions at your chest). So, single crones, we're centering you for once. In fact, we're going to skip over most of marriage and partnership entirely—at this stage of your life, if what you're doing is working, just keep it up. But, partnered crones, stick around! You may want to give your sex life, your relationship, and your self-esteem a fresh look from an older and wiser perspective.

No More People Pleasing

In my twenties, I found myself constantly making compromises in dating that I wouldn't make in any other part of my life. I didn't tolerate hate speech or explicit acts of cruelty, but I did nod politely over a terrible margarita while an attorney explained what I—a person who studied and wrote films—didn't understand about *Citizen Kane*. Then there was the time I drove from Hollywood to Venice during rush hour on a summer Friday because I felt guilty for canceling a previous date. (Los Angeles crones, you feel me. If you're not familiar with LA, just trust me that this was a stupid decision.) Anytime I complained, I was told to not be so picky. To lower my standards. To give everyone a chance. And so I did.

Why? Because I felt like I had to. Because I had been conditioned by society, my culture, my family, even my schooling to be a people pleaser. Especially when it came to men. So I contorted myself to make sure that I was pleasing to my date. And if that meant listening to an employment lawyer misdefine *deep focus*, or sitting in bumper-to-bumper traffic on the 405 on a sweltering day, so be it.

I would spend those first few dates working so hard to make my date like me that I didn't even consider *if I liked them*. Sometimes we'd reach the fourth or fifth date before I realized that I didn't want to be there. Even though I knew back then that I had zero desire to get married or have kids, I was still centering a potential partner's thoughts and feelings over my own.

Many of us felt like we had to make these kinds of concessions or compromises when we were younger. Sometimes it meant we overlooked things. Sometimes it meant we silenced ourselves. Sometimes it meant we settled. We lacked the **Wisdom**, the **Knowledge**, the **Fuck It** that we have now. Now, the only person who you need to think about pleasing is yourself.

SINGLE-MINDED

When I got divorced in my forties, I was told "not to expect much" when it came to dating. After all, everyone knows that dating is a nightmare. But dating as a *crone*? That's a curse—and one that would only grow more terrible with each passing year. The message was clear: ABANDON ALL HOPE, YE WHO ENTER HERE. But actually, dating in your crone years doesn't need to be a Dantean hellscape.

The curse of crone dating is that the pool of potential partners is (supposedly) shallow at best, so we (supposedly) shouldn't be so picky. We should lower our standards and give everyone a chance, because we don't have that many options. But as we discussed, we're too old for this kind of people-pleasing bullshit! Our high standards come from (say it with me now):

Wisdom, to know who we are
Knowledge, to understand what we want
Fuck It, to do what we please

I'm not telling you that you shouldn't date someone who doesn't tick every box on your 638-item "Ideal Partner" list. Compromise is a necessary part of any relationship, not just the romantic ones. But make sure you're not compromising the parts of yourself that you hold dear.

Now, granted, if you're *not* willing to lower your standards or settle? Then, yeah, it might be more difficult to find a compatible partner. That's always true—if you are willing to take *anything*, you're more likely to get *something*. But the beauty of crone life is feeling secure in (and by) yourself and no longer contorting yourself to fit other people's needs. For a crone, the worry isn't that you'll die alone. The worry is that you'll spend your remaining time and energy on someone who is not worthy.

But if your confidence is beginning to flag, or you're feeling like you should settle after all, then it's time to call for backup. To bring in your own personal hype person. Someone who can give you the big, inspirational speech to set your head and your heart right.

It's time to phone an imaginary friend!

Phone an Imaginary Friend

I lived alone during most of the COVID-19 pandemic and could go weeks without talking to or seeing another human. So I just came up with someone to talk to. That someone was Carrie Fisher (RIP), Patron Saint of **Fuck It**. (I spoke to her often while writing this book.) And while real friends are vital parts of every crone's life, sometimes you just want someone to remind you that you're amazing on repeat.

YOU'LL NEED

* A (physical and/or digital) picture of your imaginary friend(s)
* Tape, for displaying picture (optional)

THE RITUAL

Drop a picture of your imaginary friend on your dresser or tape one on your mirror to chat with. (Save a photo on your cell phone for when you're out of the house.) I prefer having one person, but if you want a committee of imaginary friends, no one's stopping you! And don't accidentally glamour yourself into thinking your imaginary friends are *actually* your friends. Beware talking to your imaginary friends in public. Strangers may stare when you say things like "Yes, Rihanna, I *do* deserve more," "I *am* hot, Brendan Fraser," or "You're right, Santa, I *have* been a naughty girl."

Carrie Fisher

When I was a kid, I wanted to be Princess Leia. When I grew up, I wanted to be Carrie Fisher.

The first time I saw Carrie Fisher was when I saw *Star Wars* at the Yorktown Mall. Princess Leia Organa stood out amongst the parade of (male) characters and (male) droids and (mostly male) aliens. She was demanding. She had a vicious wit. She was a hero. She was everything that six-year-old me wanted to be.

But writing is what made me fall in love with Carrie Fisher. It began with her novel *Postcards from the Edge*. The semi-autobiographical book tells the story of actress Suzanne Vale as she details her life in rehab and beyond after a drug overdose. I read it over and over, trying to decipher how she made drug addiction and family drama both emotionally resonant and so pants-wettingly funny. Her writing transitioned from semi-autobiographical to autobiographical in her one-woman show, *Wishful Drinking*, which detailed her experience with addiction and mental illness. Fisher wrote about her bipolar disorder openly, with her trademark acerbic wit.

Carrie Fisher was also a crone who brought her familiar everywhere. In the last few years of her life, she was rarely seen without her emotional support French bulldog, Gary, a perfect chonk of a dog known for his giant lolling tongue.

In *Wishful Drinking*, Fisher said when she died, "I want it reported that I drowned in moonlight, strangled by my own bra." On December 27, 2016, most outlets that reported on her death honored her wishes. In life and in death, Carrie Fisher was the embodiment of **Fuck It**.

Flying Solo

There's no law that says you have to have—or want—a romantic partner. As a crone, you have already lived half a life. You have acquired the **Wisdom** and **Knowledge** to know what's right for you. Yes, people will ask you if you're lonely, or worried about dying alone (as if having a spouse is a "Get Out of Dying Alone" card). And, sure, being single can be lonely. But you know what else can be lonely? Being in an unhappy partnership. I've been both. You don't need the power of second sight to know which felt worse.

You probably know this, but I want you to see it in print: whether by choice or by circumstance, being single is neither affliction nor moral failing. In fact, the single crone is the most powerful crone of all. She is beholden only to herself.

Befriend fifteen cat familiars! Howl incantations at the blood moon! Hex your high-school bullies! Revel in the knowledge that you, single crone, are well and truly free.

Some tips for being a crone alone:

* **Don't completely vanish.** If you're the kind of crone who doesn't require much company, it's easy to disappear into the bog. Which can make it difficult when we inevitably have to venture out into the real world. (I can clearly remember the fear I felt the first time I was in public after social distancing.)
* **Conjure a backup.** Have an emergency contact, and make sure that they have numbers or emails for your other friends and family.
* **Invoke the power of three.** Listen, I get it. Couples tend to hang around with other couples. They might forget to invite single pals. And if you've gone through a divorce? Couple friends will sometimes quiet quit you. (Ask me how I know!) But not all couples are like that, so don't automatically exclude yourself just because you're single.

* **Practice going solo.** If you're self-conscious about being a lone crone in public, practice! Go see a movie—no one's looking at you in the dark. Head out to a local tea shop or coffee house. Have dinner alone at the bar of a fancy restaurant (one of my favorite pastimes).
* **Ready your bag of tricks.** Being prepared made me feel more powerful as a single crone. Keep a basic set of tools with your other talismans. Store an extra case of water under your crystal ball. And don't forget backup batteries for your magic wand!

The Bewitching Hour

Witchcraft and sex have always been linked. Throughout history, witches have been a symbol of a woman's knowledge, desire, and power. Witches used their sexuality as a way to manifest their deepest desires. It's why they struck fear into the hearts of men. (And we still do. Except now they call us childless cat ladies, broomstick-riding man-haters, and angry lesbians.) The leaders of actual witch hunts, in which people (mostly women) lost their property or lives over baseless accusations, ginned up some *really* prurient stories about nude revelry and sex with the devil to justify their persecution. And on the positive side, a lot of neopagan and witchcraft-based religious practices really do aim to destigmatize nudity and celebrate sex.

Once you cross into cronedom, though, the fun is supposed to be over. No more demon orgies or suggestively shaped broomsticks! You're no longer menacing unsuspecting visitors with the raw and terrifying power of your sexuality. Now you're mostly turning them into stew.

This is another case in which the stories leave out a lot. Yes, aging can affect your sex life. But no matter what society tells you, my friends: crones fuck.

SUMMONING YOUR SEXUAL SELF

It can be easy to overlook the seductive nature of the crone. Even leaving aside the damaging myths about whether older women are desirable, our sexual selves really can dissipate over time, getting lost in the fog of motherhood or the haze of our careers. One moment, your sexual dance card is being punched six times a week, and seven years later you're using that dance card as a coaster. But, friends, your sexual self isn't gone—she's just lost. So below are a few ways to divine her from the darkness. Or at least send up a flare.

SPELL IT OUT

✳ The Pleasure Principle ✳

When your sexual self feels like a stranger, it can be difficult to remember what pleasure and desire feel like. The intent of this spell is to remember by making a conscious effort to get a little self-indulgent. Okay, a lot self-indulgent.

YOU'LL NEED

* Something that tastes delicious—ripe strawberries, fresh bread, chocolate, red wine, a Big Mac, whatever you'll savor the most
* Something that sounds delicious (any music that gets you in the mood)
* Your favorite romance novel or smut—this can also be fanfic, a Reddit post, something you once saw on Tumblr, as long as it titillates
* Your alone space

THE RITUAL

1. Arrange your space so it's pleasing to the eye. Start your music.

2. Close your eyes and take three deep breaths. If your brain won't shut up, remind yourself that the only thing that matters right now is you.

3. If your food smells delicious, then smell it. Take a single bite, chewing slowly, savoring it.

4. Pick up your book or other material and read a passage aloud. Speaking out loud is a better way to focus on our intention than reading silently.

5. Put your book down, then take another bite of your food. Do not read and eat! You want to give each object your full attention in order to wring out every last bit of pleasure.

6. Repeat until you're done eating . . . or whenever you feel like it. The spell is about being self-indulgent, after all.

PICTURE THIS

One of the first ways desire manifests itself is through what we see. So another way to summon our sexual selves is to *see* our sexual selves. Yes, I'm talking about nudes. Nude photos are a powerful step toward conjuring the carnal crone in all of us. Taking nudes requires time and privacy, so this ritual may require some wrangling. But isn't that always the case with summoning?

Start with plants and herbs associated with sex and romance. You can find these in all sorts of forms: essential oils, scented candles or incense, even lotions or perfumes.

* **Rose:** Encourages feelings of love and comfort, eases stress
* **Jasmine:** Boosts confidence and mood
* **Ylang-ylang:** Relaxes inhibitions
* **Patchouli:** Inspires feelings of love and lust

Incorporate them in your ritual in whatever way works for you. Try one of these:

* Begin by taking a cleansing bath that contains essential oils.
* Dab oil behind your ears, between your breasts, on your heart.
* Rub lotion on your body (do a patch test for allergies first!).
* Burn incense or candles.

When you're ready, start snapping! And don't worry so much about the result. Because it's about the process, not the product. The act of taking nudes is what summons your sexual self. The photos are just a souvenir.

A few tips for successful nudes:

* Can't cross the nude rubicon? (Nubicon?) Get naked but take a photo of *only* your face. Or make use of the magic of low light, artfully draped sheets, and other strategic concealments. Remember, what you *don't* see can be even sexier!
* Don't forget to take the necessary precautions to keep your photos secure (turn off cloud sharing!). Some phones will let you "hide" pics you want to keep so you don't have to panic when someone scrolls through your photo album.
* Hate what you see? Delete them! Again, it's about the process.
* Don't hate them enough to delete? Avail yourself of the magic of photo editing. This is fantasy, and fantasy is a natural part of any sex life!

Schedule a Playdate

One of the most notable features of my crone era is that my friends and I share sex toy recommendations like we're at a recipe swap. (Especially if there's a coupon!) Making time for your own pleasure isn't just summoning your sexual self. *It's making your desire a priority.* Which sounds like crone wisdom to me.

I'm not going to tell you how to masturbate. That would be like telling Mariah Carey how to sing. You're the artist here. But if you'd like to take your summoning to the next level, try adding a touch of sex magic to your onanistic odyssey.

Remember the basic steps of every spell? To refresh your memory:

1. Create an intention.
2. Focus on or visualize that intention.
3. Release that intention into the universe.

It's not a huge leap to incorporate this process into your solo sex practice.

1. Before you begin, form whatever sexy intention you'd like: Feel like a sex goddess! Exude greater sexual power! Reconnect to your desire! Jump-start your libido!
2. Visualize/imagine/focus on that intention while your fingers (or sex toys) do the walking.
3. When you're ready, release all that built-up energy and your intention out into the universe! (Orgasm is one obvious way to do this, but it's not required. You can choose some other mode of release, like laughing, shouting, or movement.)

Remember that you can use toys with a partner too. In our crone era we are accessing the **Wisdom** and **Knowledge** to know what we need in the bedroom, saying **Fuck It** to the idea that a partner might feel insulted or diminished by bringing toys into the mix, and using every tool available to us.

RINGING THE DEVIL'S DOORBELL (NONPENETRATIVE SEX TOYS)

The rabbit vibrator was *the* sex toy of the early aughts. It was hailed as a conjurer of orgasms, a magic wand, the foundation of every sex toy collection. Personally, I found it to be a little . . . much.

Aging can sometimes result in not being able to take a banging like we used to. That extends to sex toys. So if your old faithful has become oh painful, it may be time to find some new, nonpenetrative items of enchantment. Here are a few to add to your bag of tricks.

* **A rocket in your pocket:** A tiny, no-frills vibrator belongs in every crone's bag of tricks. Basic, powerful, portable, affordable! Easy to use alone or with a partner or with four partners. Multi-speed is a must.
* **Take a licking:** An oral sex simulator may have you speaking in tongues.
* **Walking on air:** The vibration from air pulse sex toys is provided by small bursts of air instead of contact vibration. Ghostgasms!

If penetration is the way you play, there are an infinite number of broomsticks to ride. Just be aware that you might want to start smaller—and use plenty of lube!

THE RULE OF THREE (LUBES)

You might be long familiar with lube, or you may suddenly need it thanks to the magic of fluctuating hormones and age. Either way, you can benefit from having a go-to lube at the ready for when the going gets rough. Here's a quick and dirty guide to the main types of lubes to take you from dried to satisfied.

WATER-BASED LUBES

Pros: Water-based lubes are safe for use with condoms and sex toys. Plus they won't stain your sheets!

Cons: Water-based is the least lubricating of the lubes, so it's not recommended for anal sex. Also, it may irritate sensitive skin.

SILICONE-BASED LUBES
Pros: Silicone lube is a thicker lube that lasts longer, so it's perfect for marathon sex sessions or anal sex. Plus it's not water soluble, so if you like shower sex? Make it rain!

Cons: Silicone lube will damage sex toys and (most) condoms and dental dams. It will also stain your sheets, making laundry part of your postcoital routine.

OIL-BASED LUBES
Pros: Lubes made with oil (such as coconut oil or sunflower oil) are the most powerful of lubes. Useful when you need to keep going and going—think tantric sex sessions or an all-night orgy. (Do people do still do those?)

Cons: Oil-based lubes often cause yeast infections, and some people may be allergic to their ingredients. They also damage condoms and dental dams, increasing the likelihood of rips and tears.

Looking for a little extra magic?

Try a lube with added CBD or THC. Both are cannabinoids (aka weed!), but the big difference is THC gets you high and CBD doesn't. (That also means that THC lube may not be legal in your area, so check first.) Both are supposed to help relax your pelvic muscles and increase sensitivity.

Exorcizing Your Sex Toys

Sex toys are expensive, so it's understandable if your breakup rituals don't extend to trashing your toy drawer. This purification spell is a way to exorcize the spirit of your former partners so you can have a fresh start. (Metaphysically. You may still need to disinfect the toys.) This spell is best performed in the bathroom or the kitchen, somewhere with a sink.

YOU'LL NEED

* Your sex toy(s)
* A washcloth
* A bowl of warm, soapy dish water (only mild, unscented dish soap!)
* A candle
* Salt

THE RITUAL

* Gather your items around the sink. Light your candle, then sprinkle a pinch of salt on either side of your work area.
* Dip your washcloth in the soapy water. While using it to clean your sex toy, say aloud, "I claim this toy as my own. My pleasure belongs only to me."
* Rinse the toy off, then leave it to dry. (Repeat as necessary.)
* When the toys are dry, store them as needed. Blow out your candle and sweep up the salt. No more being haunted by the past!

The Magically Vanishing Libido

Sometimes, no matter how much naked photo-taking, ritual-bath-enjoying, sexual-self-summoning you do, your libido is nowhere to be found. It might be hiding behind some of these culprits:

* **Hormones.** Fluctuating hormones absolutely affect a crone's desire. Discuss with your doctor or a trained medical professional.
* **Stress, anxiety, and depression.** When my house is a mess, my brain is a mess. Cleaning doesn't magically fix my depression, but I'm more likely to want to get dirty if the house (or at least the bedroom) is clean. You can also try leaving your phone out of spaces where you might want to get down, to cut down on anxiety scrolling and mindless, distracted clicking. These hacks won't magically cure depression or anxiety—but they might keep them from interfering with your sex life.
* **Partner problems.** If sex isn't fun, you're less likely to want it. For cis women in relationships with cis men, the orgasm gap is real: women have up to 50 percent fewer orgasms than their partners! (Nonhetero relationships aren't immune, either.) Talking to your partner is the first step to addressing the issue.
* **Sleep.** Sleep deprivation leaves a path of destruction in its wake. If you're getting enough sleep but still don't feel rested, do a sleep study. Night sweats aren't the only sleep issue that can crop up in cronedom.

Closing the Chapter

If you're someone who doesn't want or doesn't enjoy sex—maybe you never did, maybe you just feel like you're done—opting to pause or completely end your sexual chapter is a valid choice. Sex isn't the only way to be intimate.

Cuddling, kissing, holding hands, or simply sitting next to a partner are all ways to be close without having sex. Any act can be intimate if you and yours add your personal magic. If anyone gives you grief about your choices or pressures you to change your mind, remember the decision is yours. It is borne out of knowing who you are and what you (don't) want. And if they don't like it? Well . . . *fuck it.*

Love Crones

We make a million and one casual decisions every day: what grocery store to shop at, what sneakers to buy, whether to take the freeway or side streets. Real contemplation is saved for the bigger decisions: Should I quit my job and go freelance? Is this the person I want to marry? Which makes sense, obviously. Who you marry affects your life way more than your oatmeal.

As the years go by, we change. Relationships change. Life changes. But often we're too busy with the day-to-day to notice those changes as they happen. Midlife is a natural moment to reassess our romantic relationships through our crone filter. Looking back, we see the first half of our lives behind us. Looking forward, the second half of our lives stretches ahead. It's a pretty decent vantage point to ask some questions . . . and possibly gain some perspective.

✦ Let's Do the MASH! ✦

Did you play MASH (Mansion Apartment Shack House) as a kid? It was supposed to predict the future. I wanted to be a writer living in a mansion in Chicago, and now I'm a writer living in my childhood bedroom at my parents' house outside Chicago. Yikes.

The intention of this MASH-inspired spell is to give us some perspective and clarity. We'll look at who we were, who we are now, and who we want our future selves to be—both in a partnership and outside of one. This spell can be done alone or as a coven!

YOU'LL NEED

* A picture of you from your twenties
* Something to write with and sticky notes (optional)
* An envelope or box
* A visual representation of your future self. This can be as simple as scribbling FUTURE ME on a piece of paper, or you can get creative with it by creating a collage, a vision board, or drawing a picture.
* A photo of yourself now

THE RITUAL

1. Sit down with the photo of past you. On the back of the picture (or on a sticky note affixed to the pic if you don't want to write on it), write five headings: DREAM HOUSE, DREAM SPOUSE, DREAM CAREER, MY BIGGEST WANT, MY BIGGEST FEAR. Below each prompt, respond as your past self would have. Add more notes if needed.

2. When you're finished, place the photo in the envelope.

3. Take out the representation of future you. On the back, write the same five headings. Write down your current dreams to envision your ideal crone future.

4. When you're finished, place the photo in the envelope.

5. Take out the photo of current you. On the back of the picture, write seven headings: REAL HOUSE, REAL SPOUSE, REAL CAREER, MY BIG-GEST WANT, MY BIGGEST FEAR, THE BEST PART OF MY LIFE RIGHT NOW, WHAT'S MISSING FROM MY LIFE RIGHT NOW. Respond to each prompt as honestly as you can about your life today. (You'll probably need extra paper.)

6. When you're finished, place the final photo in the envelope.

7. Stand up, spreading your feet wide apart, arms stretching up and out. This is also known as standing star pose, which opens the heart. If you can't stand, just do the top half of the pose. Turn around, and repeat.

8. Tuck the envelope away for safekeeping.

9. Wait three days. Then arrange your MASH notes left to right: past, present, future. Reflect on where you started, where you are, and where you want to be. Notice the differences (if any) or the similari-ties (if any) between your past and present. Turn to your present and future. Are there steps you can take now to bring you in alignment with the crone you want to be in the future? Make notes (in your gri-moire or in your head), then return the photos to the envelope and store in a safe place. Return to this spell whenever you feel like you need a crone's-eye view of your life, using your current you responses as your past you.

The Midlife Reckoning

Knowing who you are, understanding what you want, and going after it without worrying about society's judgment can make the crone a formidable and terrifying person to be married to. I have heard many a man lament that their wife "just changed" one day and asked for a divorce. They blame it on a midlife crisis. But it's really a midlife reckoning.

As a child, you're figuring out who you are. As an adult, you test that person out, figuring out which parts of you work—and which parts may *need* work. Your crone era allows you to fully inhabit that person. This is the **Wisdom** of knowing who you are.

Our attention then turns to the **Knowledge** of understanding what we want: from ourselves, from the rest of our lives, and from our relationships. It's when we train our crone eye on our partnerships that we may realize that things we were once okay with—an uneven division of childcare or household chores, the ever-present extra emotional labor, always putting ourselves second—aren't cutting it anymore. Maybe we were never okay with taking on extra work and responsibility, but we did it because someone had to *and we knew it wasn't going to be our partner.*

That's when the **Fuck It** begins to rise. Whether in anger or exhaustion or freedom or glee, you've had it. The crone is a woman who is done putting up with shit.

So what happens next? That's up to you. But here's my story.

BREAKDOWN AND BREAKUPS

My spouse had been pleading with me for about a year to go to therapy. But what did I need therapy for? I was fine! I kept my feelings in a black metal lockbox buried seventeen feet under a lake of fire. No chance of anything escaping here!

But one day, it happened: A feeling escaped. And then another. And another. After being proudly dead inside for forty-plus years, suddenly I couldn't stop having feelings. It turns out that no matter how far you bury them, your feelings will always find a way to make it to the surface. When I found myself weeping in front of the vegan cheese at Whole Foods, I figured it was time to give therapy a shot.

Like a lot of therapy, talking things out initially made everything worse instead of better. I was summoning a lot of demons. Demons are the terrifying feeling that something in your life has to change—which is always scary at first, because change is scary. In order to exorcize them fully, I had to figure out who the demons were and how they got there. Therapy didn't just help me learn how to have feelings. It helped me understand who I was. To tap into that crone wisdom that had been promised.

Over the months that followed, I named many of my demons—which allowed me to wrestle them into submission, or at least learn to live with them. However, there was one demon who refused to stop bothering me. I spent months talking around it and over it and under it, but it wouldn't go away. One day, I addressed it head-on: *I think I'm unhappy in my marriage.* It was the first time I'd said that out loud. (It took me another year to decide I wanted to leave.)

My spouse and I had been couple goals. We were an example that it could work! They proposed on the second date. I moved in three weeks later. We got married five months after that. We had a streaming show where we told funny stories about being married. We ran a blog about eating nachos with strangers. We had been married for thirteen years and had a dog and a house! What more did I want?

I wanted to be happy. But I didn't know if that included staying married.

Looking back, I think deep down I knew I wanted a divorce. I was just terrified. I was terrified of hurting my spouse, who I did love, just not in the way that would sustain a marriage. I was terrified of telling my family and dealing with their questions. I was terrified of the friends I would lose. I was terrified about what that meant for my housing situation and my financial future, as neither of us could afford the house on our own. I was terrified of paperwork. I was terrified of losing everything and having to move back home to the Midwest, my tail between my legs.

But I was *more* terrified of being unhappy forever—and eventually that terror grew to the point that I could no longer ignore it. I was still afraid of making a choice that would hurt someone, a choice that would make my life way more difficult—but it was better than feeling like the life was being slowly choked out of me.

I knew who I was, and I knew what I wanted. And when I finally said out loud *I want a divorce*, I began making my way down the path to **Fuck It**. And I won't lie—the things I was worried about? Most of them came true. But they weren't as scary as I had imagined. (Well, most of them.) It sucked to tell my spouse I wanted a divorce, but they're now living their best life. My family adjusted. I lost some friends, but I made some new ones—and I got closer to the ones who stuck around. I had to sell my house, my finances are in shambles, and I am writing this from my childhood bedroom in the Midwest. But I have fully embraced the power of **Fuck It**. My life is my own. And that's all this crone wants.

SPELL IT OUT

✳ Turning Over a New Leaf ✳

This spell bids farewell to your past and looks to the future, celebrating your freedom and eventual rebirth. It makes use of the Wiccan idea of *widdershins*, an old Scottish word that means "against the way," or counterclockwise. The opposite of widdershins is *deasil*, which is clockwise. In Wicca, deasil is used for summoning, while widdershins is used for banishing. (It's why some consider going widdershins sinister, but it's really not. They're just two sides of a coin.)

* Salt to cast a circle
* An artifact from your marriage that's easy to rip and small enough to bury: a photo, a wedding invitation, a piece of your wedding dress, etc.
* A plant—this can be a plant you already own, a new one, or even a plant outside
* Scissors (optional)

THE RITUAL

1. Create a circle of salt that's large enough for your marriage artifact to fit inside.
2. Place your marriage artifact in the circle, then say aloud: "The past is my teacher, but no longer my guide."
3. Turn the artifact ninety degrees counterclockwise (widdershins) and repeat: "The past is my teacher, but no longer my guide." Do two more ninety degree turns, repeating the phrase with each turn, until the item is back in its original position.
4. Pick up your item, then tear it (or cut it using scissors), while saying: "Everything ends so that it may begin."
5. Take the pieces and your artifact and bury them in the soil of the plant (or outside). You are now free!

Getting Back on the Market

It can be terrifying to reenter the dating world when you've just gotten out of a long-term relationship. It's harder to feel like the wise and powerful crone wielding the power of **Fuck It** when you're sipping a vanilla oat-milk latte at the coffeeshop on one of those sciatica-punishing backless wooden stools, waiting for your Hinge date to show up.

A return to dating can curse even the most confident of crones with feelings of self-doubt. While the dating advice that opened this chapter can apply to all crones, those of you back in the dating pool after a long layoff might need an extra boost. So if you're plagued by panic or are having a crisis of confidence, here's a simple spell to psych yourself up—and not out—for a date.

✳ Pick a Card ✳

Tarot readings can be used to answer specific questions about our lives, or give us some insight into our day. But they can also be used to bring us a little extra oomph when we need it. So don't be afraid to call upon a mystical power for backup.

YOU'LL NEED

* A tarot deck

THE RITUAL

1. Visualize what energy you want to project on your date. Confident? Engaging? Cool? Flip slowly through the deck while concentrating on

your intention. Select a card that fits that vibe. Or choose one of the following:

- **The Empress.** Representing feminine power and sensuality, the Empress is an ideal addition to any date night magic.
- **Strength.** Representing not only physical strength but also courage and passion, the Strength card will set you up for success.
- **The High Priestess.** Representing intuition, the High Priestess has your back when you need to listen to your gut.
- **The Magician.** A card to remind you that you are made of magic.

2. Tuck your chosen card in your pocket, in your sock, even in your bra.

Note: Tarot cards have different meanings depending on their position (upright or reversed). The above associations are all for upright cards, so position accordingly!

THE RETURN OF THE MAGIC MIRROR

One of the downsides of being a crone who is back in the dating world is the reemergence of the Magic Mirror—you know, the voice of the patriarchy. The mirror loves to make us feel like garbage, comparing us with other women, reminding us that we're not the fairest one of all.

Of course, I was aware of the Magic Mirror's existence while I was married. I knew its message was bullshit. When I was part of a couple, it was easy to ignore the mirror. It wasn't speaking directly to me. But like all systems of power and oppression, just because it doesn't apply to you now doesn't mean it won't come for you in the future. Because once I was single again, the mirror didn't just come back—it also came up with new ways to make me undermine and second-guess myself! Not the sort of progress I was hoping for.

If the last time you went on a date was more than a decade ago, you might find yourself transported right back to your younger years, when the Magic Mirror was the loudest—and you took its message to heart. (This is going to be especially true if you're dating men, because the Magic Mirror was invented specifically to protect their fragile little egos—but any crone can fall prey to the curses of people pleasing, peacekeeping, and making yourself as small as possible to make room for everyone else.) So if you find yourself getting ready for a date and the Magic Mirror tries to worm his way in, here are some ways to respond.

MAGIC MIRROR: BE NICE!
You should agree to a second date even though you're definitely not interested.

CRONE: BE KIND.
I should say no to the date (as gently and safely as possible) so nobody wastes their time.

MAGIC MIRROR: DON'T BE DIFFICULT!
I know you're lactose intolerant, but it's practically impossible to get reservations for that fondue place! You can probably get a salad.

CRONE: STATING MY NEEDS ISN'T BEING DIFFICULT.
What's difficult is shitting myself in front of a lava pit of boiling dairy. I'm going to suggest somewhere else.

MAGIC MIRROR: BEING DIRECT IS A TURNOFF.
You can't ask them how they feel! You'll scare them away!

CRONE: COMMUNICATION IS SEXY.
I'm not a mind reader, I'm a fortune teller.

MAGIC MIRROR: OKAY, BUT *ASKING* FOR ATTENTION IS NEEDY.

Wanting them to call or text or tell you in advance if they're going to cancel or generally communicate with you is too demanding!

CRONE: I DESERVE ATTENTION.

I'm allowed to ask someone to stay in contact, ask questions, take an interest, and keep me updated, to whatever degree feels good to me. If it doesn't work for them, that's fine—we can part ways.

MAGIC MIRROR: YOU MAY NOT LIKE THEM, BUT YOU CAN CHANGE THEM!

He said *Practical Magic* was a female feelings movie, hated the all-female Ghostbusters, and, uh, calls women *females*. He needs you to teach him!

CRONE: EVEN IF I COULD, I DON'T WANT TO.

It's not my job to make better men (and it's not my job to make anyone of any gender a better person).

MAGIC MIRROR: YOU'RE GOING TO DIE ALONE.

Just sayin'.

CRONE: BUT AT LEAST I'LL DIE HAPPY—

—because I'll have destroyed you first.

MIND THE (AGE) GAP

If you're returning to the dating world after a decades-long absence, you'll discover that there's a whole new group of people that weren't there before: younger people. I don't mean younger like you're forty-three and they're thirty-seven. I mean younger like you're forty-three and they're twenty-five.

When the older partner is male (particularly in a hetero relationship), age gaps are often considered predatory, due to the uneven power dynamic between partners. That's because patriarchy skews the power scale. To some degree, *all* young women are being groomed by patriarchy to be exploited. (Sorry to be really sunny and positive!) When the older partner is a woman (or a "cougar"—thanks, I hate it), the issue is more about social judgment. You remember what we said about crones aging out of sexiness. A lot of people think there's something vaguely embarrassing about an older woman dating at all, let alone dating someone much younger.

And, look, you may not want to date someone younger! They might try to make you go rock climbing. You might have to learn about Charli XCX. But it's also an excellent opportunity to get in touch with your **Wisdom**, **Knowledge**, and **Fuck It**. Being the more experienced, self-actualized person in a relationship can give you a chance to set boundaries and express your needs in a way you may never have tried before.

I didn't know that my boyfriend was twenty-nine when he asked me out. I knew he was younger, but not how much younger. I was forty-seven, putting a full eighteen years between us. I did the math, unfortunately, and realized I'd started college before he was even born.

We went on our first date on January 1, 2020. I thought it was a fling. But then the pandemic hit, which meant if we wanted to see each other in person, it was going to have to be for a full two-week quarantine.

My ex had moved across the country, and I was finally, blessedly, alone. I finally had achieved the personal and emotional space that I had been craving for years. I wasn't about to give that up. But living out my crone-era divorcée debauchery over Zoom was getting old. So I had to figure out how to preserve my space, my sense of self, and my boundaries at a time when I couldn't just kick my boyfriend out after a date. There was no way around it: I was going to have to *communicate*.

Before he set foot in the house, we discussed the practical side of sharing space: cooking, cleaning, and various house chores. But we also had a frank discussion about our relationship. He had never lived with anyone and was nervous. I truly had no expectations—for the two-week period or the relationship—but I ended the conversation with this: *If you want this to be a relationship, then you have to be a partner.* I had spent the last thirteen years centering someone else's emotional well-being, and I wasn't willing to play caretaker anymore.

It was the sort of talk that previously would have been terrifying to me. The kind that scares people off because it's "too serious." But I had the **Wisdom**, **Knowledge**, and **Fuck It** to know what I needed and to be explicit about it—even for a supposed fling. And while this probably would have scared off some young men—and good riddance to them—I suspect his relative youth helped him be adaptable, open, and not too set in his ways. It set a precedent to simply speak up if something was bothering us. There were no misconstrued slights, no harbored resentments. We asked for what we needed in the moment instead of expecting the other person to know. It's four years later, and we're still together.

Yes, it is an age-gap relationship and there can be some imbalance. However, that imbalance usually stems from me simply having been alive longer than he has. I have the **Wisdom** and **Knowledge** of being a crone. But wielded carefully, our age imbalance can be used to strengthen our bond. And, of course, there's always **Fuck It** if anyone has a problem with that.

Maude Chardin

Harold and Maude is a 1971 film written by Colin Higgins and directed by Hal Ashby. Harold (Bud Cort) is a man in his twenties who's obsessed with death. Maude (Ruth Gordon) is a seventy-nine-year-old woman who's obsessed with life. Their paths cross when they both attend a stranger's funeral—Harold is there to observe death, while Maude is there to remind herself of life.

Maude lives exactly how she pleases. Her home is an abandoned railroad car. She plays the banjo. She frequently breaks the law, stealing everything from hearses to sick trees that she replants in the forest. Her motto is "It's best not to be too moral. You cheat yourself out of too much life." Later, her **Fuck It** is on full display when she tells Harold: "Everyone has the right to make an ass out of themselves. You just can't let the world judge you too much."

Harold can't help but be fascinated by Maude's outlook on life, which is in stark contrast to his own. And while he bristles against any kind of authority figure, he completely submits to Maude. Their friendship eventually turns to love, resulting in one of the most iconic scenes of the movie: a postcoital Harold and Maude, naked under the bed sheets while Cat Stevens's "I Think I See the Light" plays in the background.

Maude Chardin is a woman who embodies every one of the crone touchstones in full. She's wise. She's knowledgeable. And while she squeezed every last drop of life out of her eighty years, she had enough **Fuck It** to last another eighty.

Your Heart's Desire

I never imagined that I would be dating in my crone years. But then again, I never imagined much for my crone years. In my seventh-grade humanities class, we had an assignment to write our own obituary. (I know, dark.) My classmates' entries were filled with names of imaginary future spouses and children and great-grandchildren. Mine ended with "she will be mourned by her pets and her plants."

Both my teacher and my classmates insisted I would get married and have children, because that's just what people do! But even at twelve years old I knew that "that's just what people do" didn't mean it was something I had to subscribe to.

My wish for you is that you take the advice from this chapter to heart. That you let the crone touchstones guide you to a life filled with the love and sex that you desire. To find a partnership that is worthy of you. To muster the courage to make changes. And to silence the Magic Mirror and all its associates who try to tell you otherwise.

There will always be someone who will try to make a crone feel undesirable. Some mayonnaise-faced man with a head like a thumb will call you unfuckable on the internet. Because that's just what they do. But it's not something you have to even momentarily consider. To paraphrase Baudelaire: the greatest trick the devil ever pulled was convincing the world that crones don't fuck.

6

MOBILE
CRONE

When my Baba had a stroke in her late seventies, my mother rushed down to Florida, where she and my aunt helped Baba recover. Later that year, my family made our annual pilgrimage to visit her, making the drive from Illinois to where she lived on the Florida panhandle. Over the seventeen-hour drive, my mom reminded me, my brothers, and my father that Baba was still recovering from her stroke. We couldn't expect her to be moving at the same pace. We would have to be extra patient when we took her to do her shopping and her errands, as Baba didn't drive. We all (obviously) agreed. Stroke or not, Baba was nearly eighty years old. Of course she would be slowing down.

We pulled up in front of the modest low-slung ranch house in Destin right before noon. Usually, Baba would hear our car and shuffle out in her housecoat to greet us. But this year, she wasn't there. My brothers and I shared a look. Mom was right. She really was slowing down.

It was at that moment that we heard her voice calling from above. Baba was on the roof. The gutters were clogged, she explained in Russian, but there were piroshki on the counter and cold pop in the fridge.

And that is how I like to think of the crone. Assume her to be helpless and frail? She'll greet you from the rooftop of her house.

I hope that we foster crone communities as we get older. But we also need to be able to take care of ourselves. If we want to live alone in the dark heart of the woods, it'll be difficult to find a gardener to mow the lawn under our chicken-legged hut.

People are living longer and longer, but society still tends to make women feel obsolete by the time they hit their forties, if not before. So even if you've picked up this book about aging, you probably have many more years of cursing firstborns, bathing naked in the light of the blood moon, and making soup from the bones of errant travelers ahead of you. But this all depends on keeping your body agile and your wits sharp.

It's true that we cannot stave off every facet of aging. We cannot escape the toll of chronic illness. Disability and death will come for us all. But that doesn't mean we have to simply accept our fate. Because honestly, what's a better way to curse all who fear us than to live forever?

IN THIS CHAPTER, WE'LL LEARN:

* How to keep our brains and bodies active so we can keep cursing
* How to take up space and become a swole crone
* Ways to practice self-care
* Why we say we're fine—and why we shouldn't
* What to do when your body isn't cooperating

Keeping Our Wits About Us

The crone's wisdom comes from a lifetime of experience—experience that's often hard-won. Brain function can deteriorate as we get older, but we're not letting our wisdom go without a fight. Research suggests that "exercising" our brains can help prevent cognitive decline. Ensuring our minds stay active and engaged keeps our neural pathways active and our brains healthy. So while we can't cast a spell of protection to ward off every cognitive issue, it doesn't mean we can't try!

Brain exercise can include activities like reading or doing puzzles, but it also includes creative pursuits, learning a new skill, and engaging with the world around you. Don't you have something you've always wanted to try but you never got around to it? Or maybe you were scared to? Invoke the power of **Fuck It** and pick up a new crone hobby—or three!

* **Scary stories to tell in the dark:** Are you the crone who's got everyone cackling? There's no better time than now to try a stand-up comedy or improv class.
* **Role-playing games:** Gather your coven and create a campaign in Dungeons and Dragons or another tabletop role-playing game. You can live out all your crone dreams without ever having to leave the house. Also: snacks!
* **Writing in your grimoire:** Write down the stories of your childhood in your grimoire. Not only is this a great exercise in recall, but you'll have a written record of your personal history that you can later choose to share with friends, family, or—if you experience memory loss—yourself.
* **Flower power:** Take a flower-arranging class to make flower crowns and wreaths for all your moon rituals and midsummers.

Community Crone

I know, I know. I've spent an entire book talking about how the crone has spent her life putting everyone else first and finally gets to live according to her whims, and now I'm suggesting you . . . put others first? But volunteering is about caring for and investing in your community. How you show up and where you show up is all in your gnarled, bony hands.

* **Food banks/meals-on-wheels:** Nothing makes people happier than showing up with dinner. (It's also a great way to meet older crones and build community!)
* **The library:** What more natural state is there for a crone than to be surrounded by thousands of dusty tomes? (Although if the tomes are that dusty, it may be time to get back to work.)
* **Arboretums and nature centers:** Teach school children about the mysteries of the woods so that they'll grow to love and protect them as you do. Plus you might find a protégé or two.
* **Animal organizations:** If being amongst humans isn't your thing, spend your days surrounded by familiars waiting for their witches.

A Body of Work

Staying active isn't limited to just our brains. The mobile crone also needs to remain physically active. But we can't do that without first talking about the magic of the aging crone body!

Crossing the threshold into cronedom can feel like a baptism by fire—especially if you're experiencing hot flashes. As we get older, our bodies, our metabolisms, and our hormones change. Sometimes I feel like the psychological shift into cronedom is so seismic that a physical shift occurs just as an aftershock.

While not all crones go through perimenopause (and its older sibling, menopause), all crones can—and usually do—experience related symptoms. That's the magic of hormones! Whether you've ever had a period or not, fluctuating estrogen levels can cause hot flashes, night sweats, libido changes, mood swings, weight gain, and loss of bone density (osteoporosis). It can make a crone want to walk headfirst straight into the bog and disappear for good. (Plus I imagine it's cooler there.)

The physical effects of aging have a way of sneaking up on us. Our bodies are a roadmap of our years on this planet. Pregnancies, illnesses, and weight fluctuations can leave scars, stretchmarks, and sagging skin. The gravitational pull of the earth wages war against our flesh, causing various body parts to droop or jiggle. I'm not going to lie. It's a lot.

Most Gen X and millennial crones were fed a steady diet of body shaming by the media as we grew up in the 1990s and 2000s. Hating our bodies wasn't just a hobby, it was our birthright! Women were looked upon like slabs of meat, pared down to "problem areas." In our crone era, let us take it upon ourselves to make our entire existence a problem area!

The body positivity movement of the last few decades has worked to combat some of this messaging. Body positivity is all about loving your body regardless of social pressures and judgments about size, skin tone, physical ability, and so on. And if that works for you, great! However, it can still ring hollow for some—like me. I've worked hard to not hate my body, but I don't always love it. Can't I just exist in the primordial goo?

The answer is yes. Welcome to body neutrality.

Anne Poirier, author of *The Body Joyful* and the woman credited with popularizing the movement, defines body neutrality as prioritizing the body's function rather than its appearance. Your body isn't a positive thing, nor is it a negative thing. It's just a thing, completely divorced from your worth as a person. Consider yourself a human car. You can care for your body, train it, perform regular oil changes, and generally see some benefits in having it, without also having to praise or cherish it. (Maybe you'd like to live a less car-dependent lifestyle, but you also need to get to the mall.) A lot of people, especially women, have heard people saying "all bodies are beautiful," and may even believe it on some level, but don't know how to apply that to themselves. But beautiful actually isn't the most important thing a body can be! It's not really important at all!

Another way to look at it: every body is different. But every body is also the same: filled with blood and guts and organs, all stuffed into a fleshsuit. While not all of our fleshsuits look the same or will be able to do the same things, we can try to keep our individual fleshsuits in the best condition we can according to our abilities. (Grossed out by the word *fleshsuit* yet?)

Your body may not look like what it used to look like. It may not work how it used to work. It may not do what it used to do. None of that matters. I don't expect my 2004 Mini Cooper to drive the same as a 2024 model. It doesn't make it a bad car, it just means I might have to have some adjustments. Meet your body where it is now.

Let's Get Physical

Most of us have had some kind of negative experience when it comes to working out: conflicting information, confusing messaging, and dudes who believe that doling out training advice is their birthright. But until we return to the primordial ooze from whence we came, we're stuck here in our fleshsuits. Staying active in your crone era is one of the ways to keep yourself up and running (or walking, or whatever you feel capable of). Here are just a few of the specific benefits of physical activity:

* **Better sleep:** Fluctuating hormones can mess with your sleep cycle. But physical activity is proven to improve sleep immediately.
* **Better mood:** There's scientific evidence that exercise lifts your mood and helps reduce depression. Crones have earned the right to be crotchety, but it's nice to be happy sometimes, too.
* **Better balance and coordination:** Worried about falling off your broomstick in your later years? Regular exercise helps maintain your balance and coordination, so you can keep flying—and walking—straight.
* **Improved bone density:** Osteoporosis is a crone curse that comes for us all, causing bones to become brittle and break. Activity—especially weight-bearing activity—has a magical way of reversing this curse.
* **Long-term crone-ing:** Staying active helps maintain our independence—useful for crones who want to retire to a witch's cottage in the woods. (Or, like my Baba, clean your own gutters in the blazing Florida heat.)

You'll get some of these benefits from *any* amount of exercise, so don't worry if you don't have the endurance you used to, or you have reduced exercise capacity because of illness, disability, or just not feeling like it. It's better to move when you can, as much as you feel like you can. Also, throw away the notion of pursuing a "summer body" or bemoaning a "winter body." There is only one ideal crone body for all seasons: one that can continue to curse firstborns for generations to come.

Granny Weatherwax

"Granny was an old-fashioned witch.
She didn't do good for people, she did right by them."

—TERRY PRATCHETT, *CARPE JUGULUM*

Also known as "She Who Must Be Avoided" to the Trolls, "Go Around the Other Side of the Mountain" to the Dwarfs, and the Hag O' Hags to the Nac Mac Feegle, Terry Pratchett's Esmé Weatherwax is the resident witch of the town of Bad Ass. She doesn't like being called a crone, but she's the pure embodiment of crone ethos.

Granny Weatherwax is wise, but her **Wisdom** is accompanied by a quick temper and a sharp tongue. She's smart, but her superior **Knowledge** means her methods are rarely understood by those around her. She leads with her **Fuck It**, being unapologetically herself: the greatest witch on the Discworld. Her greatest asset is her total, nigh-unshakable confidence. Not to mention her withering stare.

Granny practices many styles of magic, but her main skill is the art of headology, which is quite simply getting into people's heads—for instance, it's much easier, and way more effective, to let someone *think* they've been cursed than it is to actually curse them. It's not the flashiest kind of magic, but Granny doesn't care about what her magic looks like. She cares about what her magic does. Because under her prickly, no-nonsense nature is a woman who is deeply compassionate toward the world around her and will do whatever it takes to help people—even if people don't always understand or appreciate that they're being helped.

The magic of activity is that it can be anything: Hopping on your broomstick to run to the apothecary for some mugwort is activity. Chasing after your neighborhood peahen is activity. Dancing in a grove of alder trees under a full moon is activity. But if you're looking for something more daring, invoke the power of **Fuck It** and try something new.

* **Burlesque dancing:** Burlesque is known for being an open and inclusive space for all sorts of bodies, ages, and ability levels, making it a perfect fit for crones (especially if you're still working on your power of **Fuck It**). If you use a wheelchair or have limited mobility, burlesque chair dancing (or chairlesque) can be done mostly seated.

* **Tai chi:** This Chinese martial art, characterized by deep breathing and slow, focused movements, is great for crones in wheelchairs and crones with limited mobility.

* **Aerial yoga:** Want to practice flying? This form of yoga uses aerial silks for support, so you can stretch more gently without overloading your wrists or knees—and, of course, feel like you're levitating.

* **Water aerobics:** A low-impact, joint-friendly option for all crones. In fact, most classes are attended mostly by crones, so if you're looking to find community, this is your in! Some pools will also have adaptive gear so crones with limited mobility can participate.

* **Silly little walks:** One of my favorite ways to get some exercise. A lap around the neighborhood gets the blood circulating and is also a great way to clear your head. It's also a great excuse to be a nosy neighbor. You're just on a silly little walk!

Take Up Space

Steel cages. Iron plates. Hulking chains. Grunts and groans of tormented souls, trapped within. No, I'm not talking about a dungeon. I'm talking about the weight-lifting gym.

The guidance and wisdom around women's weight lifting has been going through somewhat of a renaissance lately. To which this crone says: *it's about fucking time.* Many of us grew up in a time when all women's weight training had a caveat: *Beware, lest ye get too large!* Small was beautiful. Small was feminine. Small was the goal. Keeping women small—physically small, spiritually small—kept us in line.

Like many Gen X crones, I spent my entire adolescence on a diet. Every day was an exercise in denial as I attempted to whittle myself into nothingness. And it went on for decades. Looking back now, I wish I could tell tween and teen me that taking up space is a gift. And that celery sticks and a Diet Pepsi is not a lunch.

If you take only one thing from this chapter, let it be this: *take up space.*

As I've written in previous chapters, the world doesn't want the crone to take up space because it fears the collective power of our **Wisdom**, our **Knowledge**, and our complete and utter **Fuck It**. So the world works to make the crone small—physically and spiritually small, as it's been demanding her whole life, but now also banished to the margins and rendered invisible. Taking up space is refusing to apologize for our presence, for our body, for our power.

Weight training is the foundation atop which I have built my crone era. It has completely recalibrated my relationship with my body. It has been the most meaningful way I take up space. The simple act of putting plates on a bar helps me focus on what my body can *do* versus what it looks like. The amount I am lifting is a tangible, trackable measurement—but also one divorced from my body size and shape. Being able to easily pick up items—a heavy suitcase, a water jug, a sixty-five-pound pit bull (RIP, Olive)—makes me feel independent, powerful, capable, and present.

Now, weight training may not be for you, either for physical reasons (please be especially cautious if you have back or knee issues!) or because it just doesn't float your boat. (Though if you want to try, read on! I would love to assemble a squad of buff crones.) The important thing is to get comfortable taking up space, whether that means big muscles or just big energy. Look for movement options that let you feel like you own the room.

THE SWOLE CRONE

Weight training doesn't require that you hire a trainer, or become a gym rat (or gym possum, gym shark, or gym tardigrade), or even join a gym at all. Just incorporate some basic movements into your crone lifestyle. The exercises below are a great jumping-off point for any beginner, forming the base of a weight training routine—or an active ritual to begin your day. You'll be taking up space in no time. And as always, consult a medical professional before embarking on a workout routine.

WELCOME TO THE CRONEDOME!
A warmup routine that can also be your whole workout if you're tired.

Perambulate: Walk or jog in place for 2 to 3 minutes, until warm.

Broomstick pass-throughs: In the gym, you might use a section of PVC pipe. But at home, you can use an actual broomstick. (A mop works, too.) This exercise is a way to improve shoulder mobility and range of motion, excellent for crones who hunch over a computer all day.

1. Hold your broomstick at the level of your hips with a grip about 6 inches wider than your shoulders.

2. Raise the broomstick over your head, keeping your arms straight.
3. Rotate your shoulders to move the broomstick behind you until you feel a stretch, adjusting grip if needed. You're moving the broomstick toward your butt, but it's fine if you can't get all the way there. Hold for 5 seconds.
4. Return to the starting position and repeat 10 times.

THE CRONE ALSO RISES
A basic squat, working your quads, hamstrings, and glutes.

1. Stand in front of a chair with feet about shoulder-width apart, or slightly wider if that's more comfortable. (If you have balance issues, set your chair up in front of a countertop or something to hold onto for balance!)
2. Slowly begin to lower yourself into a sitting position, sending your hips back and bending at the knees. Hold your arms out front for balance.
3. As soon as your butt touches the chair, stand up, pressing through your heels. Repeat 10 to 12 times.

> A chair with a taller seat will be easier, while a lower seat will be more difficult. As you progress, you can lose the chair entirely!

BEGONE!
A basic push-up against a wall, working your pecs, shoulders, and triceps.

1. Stand facing a wall, with your arms straight and your palms flush against the wall, slightly wider than shoulder-width apart.
2. Move your feet back until you reach an angle you're comfortable with.
3. Bend your elbows to slowly lower your chest toward the wall, making

sure your elbows stay close to the body and don't flare out.

4. Pause, then press back up, straightening your arms. Keep your core engaged and try not to let your shoulders hunch up around your ears. Repeat 10 to 12 times.

To make this move harder, incline your body more—you can move your hands to a countertop, a low stair, and then eventually the floor!

PULLING DEMONS

A bent-over broomstick row, working your lats, hamstrings, glutes, and spinal erectors.

1. Stand with your feet hip-width apart, holding a broomstick (or a dumbbell) with both hands so it stretches horizontally across your body.
2. Hinge forward at the waist, pushing your hips back and letting your knees bend slightly. Let the broomstick hang down toward the floor.
3. Squeezing your shoulder blades together and keeping your core tight, pull the broomstick toward your chest. Pause, then lower the broomstick in a controlled movement. Repeat 8 to 10 times.

GYM CRONE SURVIVAL KIT

Heading to the gym? Keep these talismans close to hand.

* Hand sanitizer, because you don't know where those weights have been.
* Crystals, for protection or luck.
* Scrunchie, for long-haired crones.
* Hand fan, to keep cool or hide behind.
* Mints or gum, because workouts make my mouth taste like death.

* Water bottle, obviously.
* Muscle balm, because some days, everything hurts.
* Knowledge of where the nearest bathroom is located.
* Wisdom, to know when you can't hold it 'til you get home.

Self-Care Cauldron

Self-care is one of those phrases that feel like they're always trying to sell us something. Maybe because they're often trying to sell us something. Face masks and lotions and bath bombs and nail decals, calming teas and yoga mats and warming socks—the world of self-care can be overwhelming to the point that it requires its own brand of self-care.

My biggest issue with self-care is that it often comes with a hefty price tag. Like the "spa day." A spa day is a mythical unicorn. A beautiful legend that we've all heard of, something that seems like it could possibly, maybe exist . . . but I've never seen one. And I don't know anyone who has. Sure, I've had spa treatments. A hot stone massage. A mani-pedi. A seaweed scrub. But having the time and money for an entire spa day? Sure. Let me know when the Loch Ness Monster shows up.

However, self-care is still an important ritual for the crone to practice! Many crones have spent their lives prioritizing everyone else's needs over their own. So if our crone era is about turning that focus back to ourselves, well, self-care seems like a great and relaxing way to start. (And this vision of self-care won't break the bank!)

Our crone's version of self-care will cover better sleep, natural remedies for hot flashes, and a creative way to deal with anger and mood swings. But we begin with the ritual bath.

A ritual bath is a bath with a specific intent—think of it like a spell in the water. Ritual baths can be a spiritual cleanse, a healing tonic, a purification spell, or just a way to avoid the world for an hour while you leisurely soak in warm, scented water like a human tea bag. Ritual baths can be done on a budget, so they're accessible to most every crone. And sure, it's not a spa day. But you know that unicorn shat glitter all over the steam room!

A RITUAL BATH FOR EVERY WITCH

The intention of all of the following baths is relaxation. If you'd like to add an additional intention to your soak, have at it. But don't create work for yourself; the point is to de-stress!

BOG WITCH

If you can't be in the woods, then soak in the woods! Sandalwood, eucalyptus, and cinnamon combine to give this bath a woodsy smell and banish all bad vibes.

* 4–5 drops sandalwood oil
* 4–5 drops eucalyptus oil
* 1 cup Epsom salts
* 1 cinnamon stick
* Lighter or matches

Mix the oils and Epsom salts together in a bowl, letting the mixture infuse for 5 to 10 minutes. Add to bath water. Light the cinnamon stick, and wave the smoke over the tub before dropping the stick in the bathwater. Soak, and become one with the trees.

SEA HAG

Orange, lemon, and grapefruit oils combine to create a bright, citrusy scent that will have you pulling your summer caftans out of storage.

- 1 cup Epsom salts
- ½ cup baking soda
- 3–5 drops orange essential oil
- 3–5 drops lemon essential oil
- 3–5 drops grapefruit essential oil

Mix Epsom salts and baking soda together in a bowl, then add essential oils. Sprinkle the mixture into the bath as water fills the tub. Soak until it feels like you're made of pure sunlight.

SNOW WITCH
Milk and mint oil mix to create a bath that both purifies and energizes—and will leave you smelling like the winter holidays.

- 2 cups milk
- 1 cup Epsom salts
- 5 drops mint essential oil

Pour milk and Epsom salts into the bathwater. Add mint oil, then soak until you feel like a crone candy cane.

MOORLANDS BANSHEE
Lavender's power to cleanse the heart and clear the mind will leave a crone feeling like she's had a spring cleaning for the soul.

- 1 cup Epsom salts
- 15–20 drops lavender essential oil

Pour Epsom salts and lavender oil into the bathwater. Soak until you feel like a flower, ready to bloom.

YOU CAN LEAVE YOUR CLOTHES ON

You don't have to get naked to indulge in some self-care! Here are some handy ways for a crone to make self-care a daily practice. Do these right after you wake up or right before you go to bed at night.

* **Pick a card.** Pull a tarot card every morning for a preview of your day. Want to take this practice to the next step? Log your cards—and your feelings about them—in your grimoire.
* **Set an intention.** Sort of like a daily meditation—come up with an intention to guide you through your day.
* **Hex something.** Similar to your daily intention, but focusing on something that you'd like to banish, like mental clutter or feelings of insecurity. (Or someone you'd like to banish. I'm not the boss of you.)
* **Get familiar—outside.** If you have a pet, I'd hope you already have a daily care ritual for them. But playing Goth Snow White for the wildlife in my backyard is one of the ways I de-stress and practice self-care. Check out how to make crow friends on page 115, and make sure you've researched local wildlife guidelines and best practices.

GOOD NIGHT, CRONE

While ritual soaks, gentle intentions, and time spent communing with nature are excellent forms of self-care, sometimes we require something a bit more basic: sleep.

Hustle culture likes to insinuate (or outright claim) that sleep is for the weak. The internet is filled with fawning profiles of tech bros who brag that they sleep three to four hours a night. But sleep is literally one of the basic building blocks of our existence. Sleep deprivation can cause a whole host of issues: memory loss, mood swings, anxiety and depression, a weakened immune system, high blood pressure—and that's just to start. So sleep isn't for the weak. *Lack* of sleep is what *makes* you weak.

Chances are that you have had periods in your life when you didn't get enough sleep. Babies are the number-one culprit, but there's also housing insecurity, stressful jobs, and the general nightmare that life can sometimes be.

But as I began to approach cronedom, I found that I was finding my way back to the blissful ritual that is a regular, healthy sleep schedule. And then it happened. A new fighter entered the arena to attack my slumber: night sweats.

Night sweats and hot flashes are the result of the hormone fluctuations that come with aging. And for many crones, they're the first symptom of cronedom to make itself known. Night sweats do not come in like Carl Sandburg's fog on little cat feet. They roar, a veritable tidal wave of sweat. Hair plastered to your scalp, salty rivulets stinging your eyes sweat. Biblical, build-an-ark, pair-up-the-ostriches sweat.

Instead of tossing and turning in your now-swampy sheets, treat yourself to some enchanted items that will keep your bed cool and your sleep deep. And even if you're not experiencing night sweats, these are still a treat for summer sleep!

* **Cooling sheets.** They're real, and they're spectacular. Sleeping on these feels like having an assistant whose sole job is to make sure the temperature of your bed is always perfect. But instead of exploitative labor, you have moisture-wicking, breathable sheets made from natural fibers—think 100 percent cotton, linen, or bamboo (my favorite).
* **Silk pillowcases.** Silk is both breathable and slippery, making it ideal when night sweats leave your scalp feeling warm and itchy. An added benefit? Silk pillowcases are also gentler on your hair, preventing pulling and breakage. Double self-care!
* **A tower fan.** Even when my room has an overhead fan, I like a fan that focuses solely on me. (Who doesn't love a little individual attention?) Get a fan with a remote control, and you can live in bed like an eighteenth-century dowager countess with a case of the vapors.

THE MAGIC OF HERBAL TEA

Herbal teas are a cheap, easy, and quick way to practice self-care. When you are tired or achy, can't sleep, are having hot flashes or night sweats or tummy pain, or are just plain grumpy, herbal tea swoops in like a magic tonic to cure what ails you. Plus there's nothing like a giant mug of piping-hot tea to make you feel like a true and honest crone. Try one of these varieties:

* **Chamomile:** Chamomile is the GOAT of self-care tea. It's calming, makes you sleepy, and doesn't taste like dirt. (I'm looking at you, green tea.) For crones who get periods, chamomile also helps soothe the symptoms of PMS.
* **Rose hip:** Don't have time for a soothing ritual bath? Thanks to anti-inflammatory properties, rose hip tea is perfect for crones with achy bones.
* **Ginger:** If stress is making you nauseous, reach for a mug of ginger tea. Not only does it calm an upset stomach, but it helps ease night sweats and hot flashes. (And it also tastes delicious.)
* **Valerian:** Valerian root isn't just a one-way ticket to sleepy town. It also promotes deeper sleep so you'll wake up feeling more rested. As an added bonus, it helps improve bone density. We love multitasking self-care!

Up until this point, our self-care rituals have been on the soothing side, like an Enya compilation playing on repeat. But sometimes, we need a more focused kind of self-care that addresses bigger feelings. Furious feelings. Crone feelings.

Portrait of the Crone as a Pissed-Off Woman

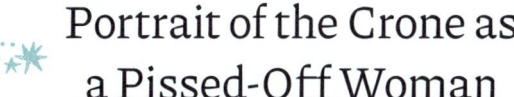

When we're feeling furious, sometimes calm, soothing vibes only make us feel worse. This ritual not only honors our feelings, but it turns them into art. And while you don't *have* to be pissed off to indulge in this act of self-care, it works particularly well if you are.

YOU'LL NEED

* Art supplies
* A large canvas, specific to your medium
* A glass of water
* A snack

THE RITUAL

* Focus on bringing every emotion you're feeling to the surface. If you find yourself crying, yelling, wailing, laughing, just let it fly. Then begin.
* Paint, draw, or sketch those emotions. You can take inspiration from anything from Munch's *The Scream* to Real Housewives gifs. Or take a black pen and scribble until the paper tears.
* When you're done and you have nothing left, sign and date your artwork.
* Drink your water and eat your snack to replenish.

The Chronic Crone

The deeper we wade into the bog of age, the more likely we are to be felled by illness or injury. For the solitary and independent crone, admitting we need help—and then asking for help—can feel like a Herculean task.

You may have heard people talk about eldest daughter syndrome—the tendency for the eldest girl in a family to be given more responsibility and expected to follow stricter rules than the rest of her siblings. This can lead to anxiety, people-pleasing behavior, and the feeling that you're responsible for everything. Eldest daughters may have lifelong trouble setting boundaries, delegating effort, and cutting themselves slack. This rings true to me, as an eldest (and only) daughter. I am THIS IS FINE in human form.

But it's not only those of us who are eldest daughters who feel this way. If you've ever been asked to take on responsibility for other people's needs or feelings—which is to say, if you are or have ever been a woman—admitting to yourself that you need help may feel like a personal failure. And even if we can admit to *ourselves* that we need help, telling someone else—someone who could actually help us—is even harder. **Why is it so difficult for crones to ask for help?** Well, it's probably some (or all) of these:

* **We're used to taking care of things on our own.** If you live in a cottage in the woods, you're obviously used to caring for yourself (and your murder of crows). But if you live or have spent a lot of your life living with a man, you've done even more work. Women in hetero marriages do more household labor than single moms. Even if they have a full-time job outside of the home.
* **We can't appear needy!** You may have been taught that it's selfish or unattractive to be "needy" (which means having any needs).
* **Or weak!** Asking for help is a very vulnerable thing to do—especially when you're already in a vulnerable position.

- * **People will judge us.** Even though you would never judge your friends in the exact same situation, you still assume they'll judge you (because you're judging you!).
- * **Or let us down.** If you've always had to fend for yourself, you might not expect people to come through for you.

DON'T BE FINE

Crones show up for each other. We'll give the food off our table and the cloaks off our backs. But when it comes to ourselves? *Oh, we're fine.*

I'm a crone, not a sociologist. But I'd posit that our predisposition toward self-abnegation stems from being told to stay small. Be quiet. Don't take up space. Growing up in the '70s and '80s, I often heard that "girls mature faster than boys"—a refrain that placed the onus of boys' bad behavior squarely in our lap. It was up to us to be the bigger person. To act as the grown-up, even though we were far from grown up. To take care of ourselves and our feelings—and them and their feelings, too. We needed help, but realized no one was coming to help us. So we learned to be fine.

Those of us cursed with heterosexuality have probably experienced a relationship in which expressing a simple need or insisting that we be treated with respect resulted in us being cast as needy, uncool, or crazy. We thought this was our only path toward love, so we shut up. *Oh, we're fine.*

As we got older, we dared not show any weakness to our male bosses at work, because there still seemed to be a burden of proof that a woman could do the job. *Oh, we're fine.* Those who became mothers were praised for being strong, for doing it all, for not needing help to the point that it felt shameful to admit you needed any. *Oh, we're fine.*

By the time we reach cronedom, we have been second-guessed, gaslit, talked over, and had our own experience questioned time and time again. *Oh, we're fine.*

But sometimes we're not.

I had signed contracts to create some big television shows that would have kept me working for the next decade and offered a small sense of security in my retirement. But completely out of left field, they fell through. An unprecedented pandemic and a divorce, a WGA strike and an animation industry gutted by CEOs have left me, after a two-decade career as a writer, with nothing. Negative nothing. My retirement plan is to fling myself into the woods and be consumed by rabid raccoons. No, I can't control a pandemic or the whims of corporate America. I would have ended up where I am right now no matter what. But I could have saved myself months of sleepless nights, my hair falling out, my destroyed savings, my poor cracked teeth, if I could have just admitted to myself that I was not fine. And then told someone else.

Let me be your harbinger. Ask for help. Or at least stop saying that you're fine.

 SPELL IT OUT

 ## The Ties That Bind

The only way to learn how to ask for things is to ask for them. We can we marshal all of our crone touchstones (**Wisdom**, **Knowledge**, and **Fuck It**) to practice the art of asking for help. But the only way to truly learn how to do it is to do it. So for this spell, you'll need a friend. Explain beforehand what the spell entails—chances are she needs it, too. The pink or yellow ribbon symbolizes friendship, while the knots are a visual reminder that there's someone to catch us before we reach the end of our rope.

YOU'LL NEED

* A length of pink or yellow ribbon (about 12 to 18 inches)
* Scissors
* A friend

THE RITUAL

1. Pick up the ribbon by each end and hold it horizontally across your chest. Have the other person carefully cut the ribbon in half with the scissors.
2. Each take a piece of ribbon and tie a knot at only one end. Exchange ribbons, then tie a knot at the other end.
3. You should each have a length of ribbon with knots tied by both of you.
4. Make a promise to each other to ask for help at least once a week for the next four weeks. These don't have to be big asks! This is just practice.
5. Each time you ask for help, make an additional knot in the ribbon, until the ribbon is full of knots. Keep the ribbon close to remind you that it's okay to reach out.

There's not enough tai chi and herbal tea in the world to stave off the possibility of becoming disabled or chronically ill. Disability activists often note that nobody's really able-bodied—they're just *temporarily* able-bodied. It's a fact of aging (and statistics) that the longer you live, the higher the odds that you become disabled or sick. But knowing it's common, verging on inevitable, doesn't make living in the reality of chronic illness any easier. Adjusting to a new normal can leave you feeling like you don't exist outside of your illness. Especially when your life shifts to revolve solely around the business of staying functional or staying alive. Here's how to try to maintain your sense of self when all your energy is focused on your health.

* **Body neutrality is your friend.** Body neutrality focuses on what your body can do and places no judgment on those capabilities. So use it to focus on your current abilities and stay in the present.
* **Focus on the small stuff.** Find small joys, make them easy to access, and return to them frequently. When a friend of mine was going through cancer treatment, she spent a lot of time in bed. So she had her husband clear out a dresser drawer and fill it with snacks so she didn't have to get up and go to the kitchen.
* **Set the scene.** Adjust your living space to your new normal, making it as hospitable as possible. This is a great place to turn to your friends who ask "what can I do to help?"
  * If you're in bed a lot, rearrange it so that you can see out a window—but also make sure that you have curtains that are easily closed.
  * If you're spending a lot of time in the bathroom, make sure it's stocked with books, breath freshener, and fluffy towels.
  * If you're using mobility aids, set up your house with clear pathways right away so you feel like you have some freedom.

* **Lean into your Fuck It.** It's not your job to be fun. It's your job to be selfish and take care of yourself.

The Rest of It

We're going to end this chapter with some rest. If you ask the Magic 8 Ball if a crone enjoys rest, the answer would be "all signs point to yes." But rest doesn't come naturally to every crone.

We learned how to be useless in Chapter 1, but taking rest is different from not doing what people want you to do. Rest is a physiological requirement for sustaining life. Lack of it wreaks havoc on every system of our body. But women are often primed to look at prioritizing rest the same way we look at asking for help: great—for other people. For *us*, rest can only be earned by pushing ourselves too hard, or staying up too late. When we feel draggy or drowsy, we apologize to other people for being tired.

Rest isn't optional, though. You can't wriggle out of it. You absolutely must engage your **Wisdom** to know that people need rest, your **Knowledge** to understand that this applies to you too, and your **Fuck It** to insist on taking a break no matter what other people expect or demand.

There is no spell. There is no ritual. Just take a nap, crones. You deserve it.

Fully Crone

So, crones: how are you feeling?

I'll tell you how I'm feeling: Proud. A little emotional. Kind of bittersweet. Exhausted to the point of near delirium. One hundred percent like a crone in all of the weird and wonderful but also cursed ways. (I may have thrown my back out while adjusting my laptop.)

In the introduction of the book, I wrote about Robert Graves, the mid-twentieth-century poet who decided to label the three faces of the Greek goddess Hecate "Maiden, Mother, and Crone," even though there was no indication in a single history book that this was factual or accurate. Some man just decided. I remember thinking, *if a Greek goddess can't decide who she is, then how can we?*

But come on, do we think Hecate listened to this dipshit? He can say whatever he wants about her, just like people can say whatever they want about you. They can expect you to behave in a certain way. They can ask you to cater to their needs. They can complain that you're not acting your age, that you're not being ladylike, that you're not being useful. That doesn't change what you owe them. It doesn't change who you are.

Whatever your path may look like, I hope that your crone years are happy, and I hope they are free. And if you find yourself lost in the forest, know that you can always return to your crone touchstones:

Wisdom, to know who we are
Knowledge, to understand what we want
Fuck It, to do what we please